T0032249

Everybody's Business

Everybody's Business

*How to Ensure Canadian
Prosperity through the
Twenty-First Century*

By Dany Assaf, Walid Hejazi,
and Joe Manget

SUTHERLAND
HOUSE
TORONTO, 2023

Sutherland House
416 Moore Ave., Suite 205
Toronto, ON M4G 1C9

Copyright © 2023 by Dany Assaf, Walid Hejazi, Joe Manget

All rights reserved, including the right to reproduce this book or portions thereof in any form whatsoever. For information on rights and permissions or to request a special discount for bulk purchases, please contact Sutherland House at info@sutherlandhousebooks.com Sutherland House and logo are registered trademarks of The Sutherland House Inc.

First edition, March 2023

If you are interested in inviting one of our authors to a live event or media appearance, please contact sranasinghe@sutherlandhousebooks.com and visit our website at sutherlandhousebooks.com for more information about our authors and their schedules.

We acknowledge the support of the Government of Canada.

Manufactured in Turkey
Cover designed by Lena Yang
Book composed by Karl Hunt

Library and Archives Canada Cataloguing in Publication
Title: Everybody's business : how to ensure Canadian prosperity through the twenty-first century/Dany Assaf, Walid Hejazi, Joe Manget.
Names: Assaf, Dany H., author. | Hejazi, Walid, 1963- author. | Manget, Joe, author.
Identifiers: Canadiana (print) 20220442762 | Canadiana (ebook) 20220442819 | ISBN 9781990823077 (softcover) | ISBN 9781990823176 (EPUB)
Subjects: LCSH: Industrial productivity—Canada. | LCSH: Ability—Economic aspects—Canada. | LCSH: Canada—Economic conditions—21st century.
Classification: LCC HC120.I52 A87 2023 | DDC 338.0971—dc23

ISBN 978-1-990823-07-7
eBook 978-1-990823-17-6

Contents

Preface

Like a hockey player skating with his head down blind to the perils of the game, Canada is about to get levelled by bigger and stronger players in an increasingly aggressive and competitive global arena. We may get up and wonder how we were blindsided and beaten at our own game. A founding member of the G7, a strong democracy, an open society with leading education and health care institutions, an energy superpower with access to the most powerful technology, yet left in the dust of the 21st century. We will all be accountable for that.

And it will only get worse once we have run out of ways to tax one another and our cupboards are bare. How will we create that new prosperity for the next generation like previous generations did for us that produced one of the world's wealthiest countries?

Well, one way would be for us to truly take advantage of the fact today we are on the cusp of the greatest revolution of opportunity and wealth creation in human history. Never before have the objective barriers to economic opportunity been lower, markets and data so interconnected, all with powerful modern technology relatively easy to get into the hands of all Canadians to exploit these opportunities. With the right framework and mindset, Canadians and humanity at large could make the gains of the Industrial Revolution look like pocket change. The efficiency and productivity of the global economic engine firing on all technology-enabled cylinders can create extraordinary levels of shared prosperity. We are only really beginning to appreciate the potential of the economic power that can be unleashed if we shift our economy from a focus on industry to a focus on the individual. The tools of productivity have been democratized and, when in doubt, our best bet has always been to just double down on ourselves and invest in the potential of the Canadian people for our next and best chapter.

The spirit of this shift was also reflected in the words of the Organization for Economic Cooperation and Development (OECD) which asked its members to "support workers rather than jobs" in their policy responses to economic recovery post-COVID-19 (OECD November 2020 Interim Report).[1] The former CEO of Microsoft, Brad Smith, acknowledged that the world is facing a "staggering jobs challenge" [and] "fundamentally the responsibility of companies and countries is to make sure that people have the skills to ensure they reap the benefits rather than suffer from the consequences of the changes unleashed . . . [and] nothing can be solved without [tech]."[2] There is a silver lining in that, with modern technology, never has it been easier or more beneficial for individuals in global communities to coordinate and connect to advance their economic, social, security, energy, and environmental agendas for themselves and their children.

The Global Village that Marshal McLuhan envisioned more than fifty years ago has gotten much smaller. Technology, travel, and

---

1   OECD, OECD Policy Responses to Coronavirus (COVID-19): COVID-19 crisis response in Central Asia. Updated November 16, 2020. https://www.oecd.org/coronavirus/policy-responses/covid-19-crisis-response-in-central-asia-5305f172/

2   Simon Jack, World faces staggering jobs challenge, says Microsoft president. BBC Online, July 18, 2020.

immigration have brought people of different backgrounds together like never before. Security is completely dependent on cooperating with allies to face state and non-state adversaries. No country can ignore the opportunity the global economy provides as a market for goods and services. Environmentally, our global ice caps are not melting because of pollution generated in Tuktoyaktuk—no walls will keep carbon emissions out of anyone's country. The war in Ukraine has also reminded us all of our energy vulnerabilities—nothing can be accomplished and no progress made while freezing in the dark. But the economic opportunity of this age was also summed up by India's Prime Minister Modi in his response and advice to President Putin to end the war in Ukraine because "today's era is not an era of war."

Canada is a prosperous, peaceful country that is respected globally, and Canadians are the envy of much of the world. We are one of the most diverse nations on earth, uniquely poised to capitalize on the modern technology-enabled global economy.

Yet we see storm clouds gathering.

The sources of prosperity that have driven Canada's success over the past 150 years will diminish in the future, and a continued reliance on these traditional economic drivers will undermine Canada's prosperity as well as its social and environmental character. These challenges require significant changes in public policy, business strategies, and individual economic engagement.

In 1967, on the country's 100th birthday, we had a lot to celebrate. We were the world's ninth largest economy, an impressive achievement for a country of only 20 million. Yet fifty years later, we had fallen to 16th place. Projections have Canada dropping to 25th place over the next fifty years, surpassed by Mexico, Thailand, Nigeria, Vietnam, Iran, and the Philippines, among others. We also ranked third in the world in terms of income per person, behind only Switzerland and the United States. By 2017, we were in 15th place and we continue to fall. Few countries have been blessed with the natural resources that we have. They have had to compensate and try harder, and the digital world has allowed them to flourish. We grew complacent with our natural riches, and now risk being left behind in the new economy. We know that what got us here will not take us there.

This book is the realization of a spark that was ignited in Toronto's Air Canada Centre in 2014. The Toronto Maple Leafs were playing the Boston Bruins. In the stands, two friends were watching with their fourteen-year-old sons. Over cups of Tim Hortons coffee, the dads were engrossed in a conversation, not about who was going to win the game (the Leafs won), but about the future of Canada. Like the Leafs, who hadn't won a Stanley Cup since 1967 (on Canada's 100th birthday), the Canadian economy felt like it had been adrift for a long time. What will Canada look like on its 200th birthday? What is motivating our national sense of purpose? What will galvanize us in this century to work for something greater than ourselves, to create opportunity for all Canadians to reach their potential, and to provide an unrivalled quality of life?

Like many Canadians, we held a strong conviction that Canada had unfulfilled potential and its best days could lie ahead, but also felt that we need a revival of purpose, consensus, and vision to propel us higher. In such a competitive world, we needed to become more excited by the idea of winning than worried by the fear of losing.

The two dads were Dany and Joe. They soon brought in Walid, a trusted friend and outspoken accomplished professor, and this book idea was born. It is also an invitation to you, the reader, to take part in a broad, inclusive conversation about the country's future.

This book offers a unique perspective that is based on conversations and extensive interviews with over 100 Canadian thought leaders, and feedback from more than 500 executives and 2,000 highly diverse graduate students from the Rotman School of Management's MBA program and the Munk School of Global Affairs. We recommend credible paths forward, and new approaches that will reduce Canada's dependence on historic drivers of prosperity. The path forward focuses on five areas: people, tools, materials and resources, capital, and markets. And these all need to operate within a frictionless ecosystem that enables people to achieve their true potential.

The COVID-19 virus brought the world to a halt, bringing both crisis and opportunity. While certain industries were hit hard, many found innovative ways to adapt. In Canada, it is estimated that approximately 25 percent of working Canadians have begun new jobs completely unrelated to what they were doing before the pandemic.[3] The number of new businesses created in the United States, the United Kingdom, France, Germany, and Japan in 2020 was greater than the previous year. While economies suffered worldwide, the *digital* economy got a dramatic boost. The words of a *Wall Street Journal* article summed it up well, "The Coronavirus destroyed jobs. It also created entrepreneurs." And in the words of one such new entrepreneur, "The pandemic [helped] me blossom [and] pushed me to do something I wasn't really ready for."[4] A recent global poll found that four-in-ten people who started a business in the last two years

---

3   Perlita Strohm, CBC News website, March 14, 2021. https://www.cbc.ca/news/business/career-job-changes-pandemic-1.5935256

4   Kim Mackreal, In the Covid economy, laid-off employees become the new entrepreneurs. *Wall Street Journal*, November 18, 2020.

said it replaced labour force inactivity (not working or laid-off), while one-third continued to work at another job and one-quarter quit to start their business.[5]

While the unprecedented potential and access that modern technology provides is apparent, the path to harnessing and deploying this potential remains unclear. The speed and degree of change has caused anxiety for many, and some politicians have exploited that anxiety to divide people, providing simple narratives that pit us against one another. Many of these narratives draw upon an outdated paradigm of tribalism. With the unique nature of our era's challenges and opportunities, today we should view all of humanity as our "tribe" to best survive and thrive.

Canada has benefitted from strategic historic relationships and its wealth of natural resources. Looking ahead, our future success will require us to expand our strategic relationships and maximize the tools that modern technology offers. We need a new economic narrative. It's time to make the business of the Canadian economy "Everybody's Business." And yes, that means you; we all have an important role to play in seizing the promise of our time and be provided the opportunity to blossom and bloom, rather than be blindsided, in this 21st-century economy.

5   See Ipsos Report, July 22, 2022.

1

Winds of Change: Geopolitical Shifts and Opportunities

I have one love—Canada; one purpose—Canada's greatness; one aim—Canadian unity from the Atlantic to the Pacific.

—John Diefenbaker

"There is no question that people are facing anxiety because of a changing economy and rapid technological change. We understand that many families are worried about their future and their children's future. Even though Canada has seen tremendous economic growth over the past few years, that growth has been unevenly shared. As politicians, we must acknowledge these concerns and anxieties and work to allay them." This was a quote from an email interview with Prime Minister Trudeau pre-COVID-19. Little did he, or we, know what was in store. The pandemic only poured fuel on the fire of these anxieties and accelerated the pace of change. A recent Ipsos Report found, "As Canadians we should continue to be concerned. Economic stability underpins a strong society. However, Canada's 'citizen sentiment,' measured via the Ipsos Disruption Barometer (IDB), was already on a downward trend that started in September of 2019. Prior to the pandemic, we were already hearing from Canadians that they felt they were 'falling behind.'"[6] Welcome to the future.

The question is how to allay these anxieties while seizing the new opportunities offered. We live in turbulent times. There is a global shift towards populism. Protectionism is on the rise. Trade discussions are heated, and full-blown war has returned to Europe. Understandably, we are worried what the future will bring for our children.

As Ed Luce wrote in *The Retreat of Western Liberalism*, President Trump and his America First agenda were not the cause of such sentiments, but a reflection of a trend. He also predicted that this trend will likely not reverse any time soon. Prior to invading the Ukraine, Russian President Vladimir Putin had already announced that liberalism has "become obsolete."[7] And there were a surprising number of people in the West who seemed to agree.

There is also another perspective coming out of the West which was captured by Chrystia Freeland, Canada's Deputy Prime Minister and Finance Minister, in a speech to the Brookings Institution of a values-based global trade regime where trade is prioritized with like minded friends and reduce dependence and trade with autocrats. This approach has also been referred to as "friend shoring" and advocated by other leading voices such as Janet Yellen, U.S. Secretary of State. Minister Freehand see this "change represent[ing] an economic opportunity for Canada".

---

6   Ipsos Report, Inflation is Canadians' top concern—Here's what you need to know. May 12, 2022.
7   Lionel Barber, Henry Foy, and Alex Barker, Vladimir Putin says liberalism has "become obsolete." *Financial Times*, June 27, 2019. https://www.ft.com/content/670039ec-98f3-11e9-9573-ee5cbb98ed36

For the first time in decades, Canadians, and even Americans, are grappling with the fear that the next generation will be worse off than the last. This issue of future economic prosperity is one of the great challenges of our time. The forces of change are only accelerating with COVID-19, and relentless technological progress has the potential for social and political upheaval. Dean Connor, former CEO of Sun Life, put it this way, "what's interesting about Covid, is a lot of the technologies and services have been designed, built and available before Covid. It's not about invention, it's all about adoption. That phrase, necessity is the mother of invention, the better line I think for Covid, is necessity is the mother of adoption. With Covid, there's been this massive acceleration in adoption of existing technologies."

We can see that beyond these dark clouds, reasons for optimism remain. We are on the cusp of the greatest potential for individual opportunity and wealth creation in human history. Thanks to modern technology, the barriers to business and prosperity have never been lower, nor markets so connected. And remote collaboration may actually increase innovation, tapping into what has been called "the collective brain." There is opportunity for literally everyone to unleash their energy, ideas, passion, and productivity and do business directly with almost anyone globally. And there is the potential for this wealth to be shared more broadly than it is now. Our collective responsibility is to ensure that every Canadian has the opportunity to tap these opportunities.

The movement towards populism and isolationism presents Canada with a unique opportunity, said Dominic Barton, Canada's former Ambassador to China and former global managing partner of McKinsey. "If we can hold our nerve," he said, "I think that can be a very big source of advantage as we're moving through it." But it's not enough for Canada to just assume that it will be a beneficiary. Moments of upheaval can present jump-ball opportunities for new players to get the ball. Extended periods of stability can make it difficult for new players to get in the game.

"We are a small country in a large world," he said, "and no matter how protectionist or not it's going to be, we are going to rely on exporting our capabilities or . . . being able to participate in global markets."

At the moment, natural resources are our largest export, but it's not something we can rely on for the future. "We do have natural resources that are a source of prosperity for us," said Jean Charest, former Quebec Premier. "It's a matter of balancing that out, of understanding that we need to be prudent in the way we manage our natural resources because it's a commodity and we are not going to be controlling the price."

Canada needs to focus on its strengths, Charest said, while recognizing that new areas such as artificial intelligence are the future. He said the commercialization of AI was happening more in the United States than in Canada. "If we are serious about AI, then we need to put a strong focus on commercialization."

Right now, that focus isn't there. There is a sense of complacency in Canada: things have always been good and somehow they will always remain that way.

"We have a social experiment here that works better than any place in the world," said Egizio Bianchini, executive vice chairman and a director of Ivanhoe Mines. "And I would defy anybody to tell me differently." He noted that Canada flourished because of a strong economic base. "Now that economic base is deteriorating. At a minimum, it's not growing. On a per capita basis, it's deteriorating.

It's not going to keep up with the population. We need to address the economic issues in this country first, or we run the risk of our social experiment falling apart."

History is filled with examples of countries that have transformed themselves. After the Second World War, both Japan and Germany turned from the ashes of war into powerhouses in the technology and automotive sectors and remain among the world's most influential economies. Then we watched Singapore and South Korea transform their economies. And today we see countries like Bangladesh grow its GDP eightfold since 1990. In 1984, Bangladesh's exports were $34 million; in 2022 they were $34 billion. There are still problems—poverty remains an issue—but Bangladesh isn't far from where South Korea was in 1975. Although there are a few examples of this kind of transformation in Canada—the federal government's Superclusters initiative and successful incubators such as the Toronto Metropolitan University's Digital Media Zone—there aren't enough to transition the national economy to the digital age.

Estonia is another country that essentially reset its economic DNA. Estonians had their passions crushed by the communist philosophy, suffering under the seductive but senseless theory of *from each according to his ability, to each according to his need.* There are very few human beings, when they have put their heart into something, who don't like to be rewarded and recognized for their efforts. In many ways this is the essence of our common humanity: to do and be seen to be doing, to provide the best we can for ourselves and those we love, and to contribute to our community and know our existence mattered.

After its independence from the Soviet Union, Estonia was able to set its own future course and took full advantage of the opportunity. The project the country embarked on was called e-Estonia, which transformed the country into a digital society. A *New Yorker* article stated,[8] "Its government is virtual, borderless, block chained, and secure. Has this tiny ex-Soviet nation found the way of the future? The normal services that government is involved with—legislation, voting, education, justice, health care, banking, taxes, policing, and so on—have been digitally linked across one platform, wiring up the nation."

The country is an object lesson in innovation. "We believe that innovation happens anyway," said Viljar Lubi, Estonia's Deputy Secretary for Economic Development. "If we close ourselves off, the innovation happens somewhere else." This mindset has transformed the country. "Previously, Estonia's best-known industry was logging," Lubi said, "but Skype was built there using mostly local engineers,[9] and countless other start-ups have sprung from its soil."

According to the BBC, "The Estonian capital Tallinn has some heavyweight tech credentials. Skype video calling was invented there a decade ago and all children are taught computer programming at school. Now it is a hi-tech haven for hundreds of start-ups, from Garage48, an event aimed at turning an idea into a working service or prototype within a weekend, to Stigo, the inventor of lightweight, electric scooters."[10] It has been called the next Silicon Valley.

Visionary leadership in Estonia allowed it to shed its past and create future policies that enriched its people. Innovation flourishes across

8 Nathan Heller, Estonia, the Digital Republic: Its government is virtual, borderless, blockchained, and secure. Has this tiny post-Soviet nation found the way of the future? *The New Yorker Magazine*, December 18 & 25 Issue.

9 https://wiki.p2pfoundation.net/E-Estonia

10 BBC Online, Tech. Estonia's hi-tech haven: From SkyPE to scooters. February 23, 2014. https://www.bbc.com/news/av/technology-26255966

the country. Estonia's platform allows people from around the world to work within Estonia electronically, an incredibly innovative and futuristic approach. Having deployed a digital society, bureaucracy has been minimized and innovation and productivity enhanced.

The managing director of the e-Estonia Briefing Centre, Liina Maria Lepik, said, "Estonia has never had remarkable natural resources other than forests covering 50 percent of the land. But we may consider our best natural resource to be the people on the ground."

Other countries and organisations like the IMF recommended that Estonians create a state no different from the rest. "Our young and forward-thinking government was bold enough to decide otherwise," Lepik said. Prime Minister Mart Laar and most of his ministers were then in their thirties, and understood the benefits of unleashing personal potential, possibly the result of years of Soviet rule, where individual potential was stifled.

In 1994, the Estonian government created the Estonian Information Policy, which agreed on a set of forward-thinking core principles. It stipulated that individuals were the owners of their personal data, that *everyone* should have access to the internet, and the digital society would be built as a public–private partnership. "Pretty forward-thinking of the people coming from an authoritarian society, would you agree?" Lepik said. "And it was twenty-five years ago."

Estonia reset its game board and is now a bastion of technological innovation. It has shed its historical economic drivers and embraced a completely forward-looking model of prosperity. There are some lessons for Canada in Estonia's example.

"Canada has the good fortune of being blessed with abundant resources," said Elvis Picardo, portfolio manager at Vancouver-based asset manager Luft Financial. "Estonia had to go digital after gaining independence from the Soviet Union in 1991 because it was the cheaper and more efficient option. Canada probably lags behind Estonia in terms of most digital economy metrics like percentage of population with internet access and services that can be accessed online. More needs to be done to encourage large-scale adoption of technology." Picardo recommends tax breaks for studying technology, development of more centres of tech excellence, and the creation of more tech-focused universities that will foster more start-ups and a culture of entrepreneurship.

Lithuania, another former Soviet-controlled state, offers an example on a smaller scale. A woman named Inga with a passion for shoes and a desire to create an environmentally responsible business launched BureBure Slippers.[11] She uses felt and "cruelty-free" wool to create handmade footwear.

Inga remembers her childhood in communist Soviet-occupied Lithuania. "I grew up in Lithuania that was occupied by the Soviet Union. If you can't imagine what this means, think about life in its current analog—North Korea. In Soviet Union people built buildings that all looked exactly the same. Passersby wore clothes and hairstyles, which never went out of fashion. Everybody would buy boring grey shoes because this was the only model produced in state factories. I can't get rid of those memories of identical shoes that stood on the shelves in dark and dusty shoe shops. They looked just like soviet soldiers—sad and grey. The Soviet Union was a country where creativity and individuality were sacrificed for the sake of a predictable society. Mass production of lifeless, boring items was a must."

11 https://burebureshoes.com/pages/how-did-it-start

Modern technological progress allowed her to take her simple childhood love of drawing princesses to selling her slippers online, made from wool from her family's organic farm. She connects to worldwide markets and her customers invisibly and almost frictionlessly over the internet and even personal electronic devices. Inga is an example of how to turn your passion into a viable 21st-century business.

Consider also the example of Kenya and M-Pesa and what this mobile banking device has done to unleash the economic potential of Kenyans and others in Africa. In the past, the Kenyan government considered mobile phones a threat to state-owned landline telephone monopolies and initially objected to the introduction of mobile phones. It worried about the loss of revenue and the erosion of state power.

However, in Kenya, just like everywhere else in the world, mobile phones were quickly adopted. They created a consumer-driven business model that provided both easy access to low-cost handsets and a new low-barrier, frictionless business opportunity for any seller or potential seller of goods or services. Professor Juma from Harvard's Kennedy School observed, "The introduction of mobile money transfer services expanded businesses through the creation of transaction kiosks across the country. Mobile technology started as a service but ended up becoming the infrastructure upon which new businesses such as M-Pesa were founded, a service that has inspired variants around the world. The industry, especially through smartphones, has become a hotbed for creativity and a source of inspiration for young innovators and entrepreneurs."[12]

---

12 Calestous Juma, What innovation and technological disruption really means for Africa. May 5, 2017. Quartz Africa. https://qz.com/972157/what-innovation-and-technological-disruption-really-means-for-africa/

As Precious Lunga, a leading African entrepreneur and founder of Baobab Circle, a health technology company employing AI to provide consultations to Kenyan and Zimbabwean patients, wrote in the *Financial Times*: "Access to mobile phones in [Africa] is now virtually ubiquitous. There are places where there's still no running water, but you can stream a video."[13]

Estonia, Lithuania, and Kenya—three different stories of passion and potential. The question is how can we unleash the passion and potential of every Canadian who is crazy about shoes or have innovative ideas about scooters or video calling.

"Canada is fabulous place to live," said Tiff Macklem, now Governor of the Bank of Canada. "It's rich, inclusive, harmonious. We have space, clean water and air, energy, and it's a safe country, too." "Unlike many other countries, we did what was right and hence have avoided the conditions that give rise to populism. These things do not create jobs and wealth. Canada is now at a crossroads. Natural resources have created wealth in the past, but this will not be the same source of growth in the future that it has been in the past. But going forward, we do have a problem, and that's complacency."

The Path Forward: People. Tools.
Materials and Resources. Capital and Markets.
And a Frictionless Ecosystem

Where can we find the keys for economic opportunity and prosperity in the 21st century? Green shoots are apparent with the example of Toronto

---

13 David Pilling, African economy: The limits of "leapfrogging." *Financial Times*, August 13, 2018. www.ft.com/content/052b0a34-9b1b-11e8-9702-5946bae86e6d

becoming the fastest growing tech hub in North America especially as the United States has introduced more restrictive immigration laws. Since 2013, the number of tech jobs in Toronto skyrocketed from about 148,000 to 228,000 in 2020, an increase of 54 percent.[14] Today Toronto ranks number 3 as a tech job hub behind only Silicon Valley and Seattle and has created the most tech jobs in North America over the last five years. [15] We need to continue to play to our strengths.

In the *Globe and Mail,* former chairman of Research in Motion (Blackberry) Jim Balsillie wrote, "Immigration, traditional infrastructure such as roads and bridges, tax policy, stable banking regulation and traditional trade agreements are all 19th and 20th century economic levers that advanced Canada's traditional industries, but they have little impact on 21st century productivity."[16]

Nations and individuals can no longer rely on multinational companies to provide long-term secure jobs. It was a model that served many, especially in the Western world, in the 20th century. We need a modern and frictionless economic platform to provide each of us with the tools to engage and navigate a more personal economic journey. "Technology is the enabler, people are the true transformers," says Dr. Rola Dagher, Global Channel Chief, Dell Technologies.

Consider how Uber uses technology to connect resources (cars) with data (real-time customer demand) and people (drivers and passengers). It puts otherwise-idle car capacity to work for the benefit

---

14 H. Cooper and D. Bank, Toronto is emerging as a tech superpower as immigrants choose Canada over the US, *Business Insider,* July 30, 2020.

15 https://www.cbre.ca/press-releases/toronto-moves-up-to-3-spot-in-cbres-2022-tech-talent-rankings

16 Jim Balsillie, Empty talk on innovation is killing Canada's economic prosperity. *The Globe and Mail,* March 17, 2017.

of consumers who need to get from point A to point B most efficiently. And while the relationship between Uber and drivers will need to evolve, along with many similar relationships in the Gig Economy, there is no doubt that Uber does allow people to be more productive economically and socially. It is a more efficient transport model to get to that client meeting, a child's hockey game, or a piano lesson. The rise of the sharing economy now extends beyond idle cars to cloud computing, apartments, homes, and condominiums.

The basic building blocks of productivity and wealth creation at any time and place in human history required are the same—*people, tools, materials, resources, capital and markets, operating within a frictionless and open economic ecosystem.* The question for each generation is: What do the ingredients of personal productivity look like in their time?

1. **People:** Today's productive and innovative people literally come from anywhere. Societies need to remain open to attract a pool of new and diverse players. The greatest cities in the history of humanity have always been characterized as open, welcoming, and diverse, attracting the best and the brightest. And their decline has always been followed by a society that became closed, divided, and insular. We have no idea where the next generation of history-altering innovations will come from. We close our doors at our own peril. The Canadian economy, to be modern, vibrant, and successful, needs to send a clear message to the global talent pool: "If you have the energy and ideas, come to Canada and put yourself, and us, to work." This also includes things like ensuring people are always healthy enough to work and have the skills, education, and knowledge to be relevant and productive in the 21st-century economy.

2. **Tools**: Modern tools that enhance productivity are key to growth and should be made available as widely and deeply as possible. In the past, it was railways, waterways, and highways that moved goods. Today this includes the digital highway, with high-speed broadband and ubiquitous wireless access and digitally literate individuals and businesses. As noted, Uber operates one of the largest transportation undertakings without owning a single car. What it needed were computers, software, and mobile access to the internet. This is also the case with Airbnb and a host of other internet-based businesses. Today, ubiquitous mobile internet access and the tools to access it are the basic building blocks for many businesses. Think of the internet as the equivalent of being able to get to work. The world continues to invest trillions of dollars in public transport to make sure workers can get physically to their job site. The logic is the same in the digital economy where we log in, rather than, drive in to work.

3. **Materials and Resources**: Access to materials and resources will continue to be vital, including rare earth minerals used to manufacture future essential parts of many high-end tech devices, such as cell phones and electric cars. However, so too will the efficient extraction, processing, and utilization of our resources in environmentally conscious ways. In the words of Mick Davis, the former CEO of Xstrata, "ESG imperatives will override anything."[17] We want to produce energy in a manner that does not destroy our most important economic platform, the planet. Being environmentally conscious can create wealth too. Clearly

---

17 Eric Reguly, Dirtyco to Cleanco: How environmental pressure is shaking up the mining industry—and will soon reshape it. *The Globe and Mail*, February 5, 2021.

conserving, recycling, and reusing are some of the most effective cost-cutting measures available to any business willing to take the time and effort to implement. But Putin's invasion of Ukraine demonstrated how fragile and complicated these goals are. Facing the spectre of reduced Russian gas supplies, several countries once more turned to coal and chopping down trees. Humans are hard wired to never let their children freeze in the dark.

4. **Access to Capital and Markets**: No commercial endeavour has meaning without ultimately being able to realize the fruits of hard work. Therefore, access to the biggest pool of customers for your product or service is crucial, and the opportunity to connect with a paying customer from anywhere is always most welcome. To nurture, grow, and fund great ideas, we also need the broadest possible access to capital and potential investors. In fact, funding is a top barrier to starting a business in most countries.[18] We don't get a good deal on a mortgage from a Canadian bank because of our Canadian passport, it's because of other capital options and competition for mortgages.

5. **Frictionless Ecosystem**: For all people and businesses to pursue their passions, creativity, innovation, and economic opportunity, there must be a friction-free ecosystem that promotes rather than impedes their efforts. While it is critical that governments be responsible to ensure the best overall social and economic outcomes for society, unnecessary bureaucracy and red tape, as defined in the 21st century, must be eliminated.

---

18 Ipsos Report, Untapped Potential, Entrepreneurialism in Inflationary Times: A 26-Country Study, July 2022, see https://www.ipsos.com/en/global-advisor-entrepreneurialism-2022

The question for us is this: How do we activate and optimize these key pillars of the modern economy to unlock maximum opportunity and prosperity for everyone in the 21st century?

Canada is "addressing its systemic economic challenges by shifting away from traditional resource dependence and taking steps to diversify its trading partnerships," said Mark Machin. He is the former CEO of Canada Pension Plan Investment Board, one of the world's biggest dealmakers. "What's more, Canada is aggressively developing idea incubators to ensure it captures pre-eminence in fields like AI and other drivers of future economic growth."

While social and political enlightenment are pillars of a country's quality of life, history has often shown that progress on these fronts is futile without economic opportunity and security. It has been well documented that diverse perspectives and inclusion are fundamentally linked to economics.[19]

The Canadian success story will come under strain, and this generation needs a new vision and framework to propel Canada into the future and keep its promise alive for a new generation.

19 Bessma Momani and Jillian Stirk, Diversity dividend: Canada's global advantage, centre for international governance. 2017. https://www.cigionline.org/static/documents/documents/DiversitySpecial%20Report%20WEB_0.pdf

2

Taking Stock:
Conservatism and Innovation

I can't understand why people are frightened of new ideas. I'm frightened of the old ones.

—John Cage

Canada is a prosperous, peaceful, and diverse country, a beacon to the world in many ways. We have largely avoided the level of turmoil that some other Western democracies have recently experienced. The election of Donald Trump as U.S. President and the Brexit vote in the United Kingdom were examples of nationalist sentiment, and a retrenchment in both trade and immigration policies. Openness to trade, investment, and immigration have delivered enormous benefits to countries worldwide, economically, politically, and socially. Since the 1960s, extreme poverty globally declined from over 80 percent to around 10 percent[20] and in the period from 1990 to 2015 alone;

---

20 Peter Beaumont, Decades of progress on extreme poverty now in reverse due to covid. *The Guardian.* See https://www.theguardian.com/global-development/2021/feb/03/decades-of-progress-on-extreme-poverty-now-in-reverse-due-to-covid

almost 1.2 billion people were lifted out of poverty.[21] The 21st-century economy can reward such openness like never before, and Canada is poised to take advantage of the new economy with its educated, diverse, and technologically skilled population.

This economy, however, needs to prioritize and ensure better access to the tools of modern productivity and to empower and reinvest in its people. This new reality was captured in one Instagram story posted by Drake. "Can the mayor of Pickering set up some stronger wifi towers so @boi1da can be able to send me all his newest beats?? Trying to cook up. Thanks.—Drake."[22]

But first we need to assess where we are at. For example, while many countries experienced tremendous difficulty during the Great Recession of 2008, Canada fared relatively well. The economic impact was milder, and we recovered much more quickly than our trading partners. The key reason for this steady performance was the resilience of the Canadian financial sector, which has been ranked as the soundest system in the world by the World Economic Forum over the past decade.[23]

This is the upside of our inherently conservative national character. The downside is an aversion to risk. And almost all innovation involves risk. George Bernard Shaw said, "The reasonable man

21 H. Kharas and M. Dooley, The evolution of global poverty, 1990 to 2030. The Brookings Institute, February 2022.

22 Derick Deonarain, Drake reaches out to Pickering mayor for better Wi-Fi after internet woes with producer. CBC News, August 01, 2019. https://www.cbc.ca/news/canada/toronto/drake-reaches-out-to-pickering-mayor-for-better-wi-fi-after-internet-woes-with-producer-1.5232594

23 See https://www.canada.ca/en/news/archive/2013/09/world-economic-forum-ranks-canadian-banks-soundest-world-sixth-consecutive-year-770139.html

adapts himself to the world: the unreasonable one persists in trying to adapt the world to himself. Therefore, all progress depends on the unreasonable man."[24] We are the world's Reasonable Man, but in order to survive and flourish in the 21st century, we need to become more "unreasonable."

John McCallum, former Canadian Minister of Immigration, said Canada has not been an innovation leader. "I am not sure anybody has a magic bullet to solve it and I don't know quite why," McCallum said. "It might be our proximity to the United States and that a lot of our economy is what you might call branch plant economy."

However, perhaps our economy did not fare as well in the COVID-19 crisis because Canadians are not risk takers and tend to take a middle path. The dynamics of a pandemic are different than a financial crisis because its impact is so immediate; each day, lives are literally on the line. In this situation, we needed a different mindset, bolder, more decisive, and we need to be prepared to take risks. The United States bet big on project Warp Speed to develop vaccines and then immediately proposed a $2 trillion transformational renewal of its infrastructure. The U.S. National Institute of Health established a $500 million "Shark Tank" like competition—the Radx program—to encourage all Americans to develop innovation-based approaches to the pandemic.[25] Boldness seems to be in their DNA, and these initiatives happened under a Republican and then Democratic party regime.

24 George Bernard Shaw, *Man and superman: A comedy and a philosophy* (Vol. 11). 1903. Brentano's.

25 U.S. National Institute of Health. https://www.nih.gov/research-training/medical-research-initiatives/radx/radx-programs

A common theme among those we interviewed for this book was an acknowledgement that Canada must become more innovative, and not enough has been done to move the innovation needle. In fact, a recent global poll found that in Canada lack of interest was a top barrier to entrepreneurship and starting a business with lack funding and access to capital coming in second.[26]

"The gap is getting much bigger and it's happening at a quicker pace," said Jerry Dias, former national president of Unifor, Canada's biggest private sector union. "So it is going to require some dramatic overhaul of the economy in order to achieve the type of opportunities where everybody is in a situation where they can benefit."

Canada's strategic location next to the United States has resulted in an enormous demand for Canadian exports. Given its proximity, size, shared culture and history, the United States is a relatively easy market for Canadians to do business with. This has made the United States Canada's largest trading partner, taking three quarters of Canada's exports. Historically, it has also bred complacency and left us ill-equipped to compete in the brutally competitive, rapidly evolving global technology sector. Where does a risk-taking mindset come from?

Canada and the United States have almost identical inputs: a wealthy, well-educated, sophisticated society that wants to succeed in a capitalist system. But the results differ substantially.

"Canadians, when they're in Canada, are a little more reserved or conservative when it comes to taking big bets," said Brandon A. Lee, Consul General of Canada in Seattle. "This is where if you look at

---

26 Ipsos Report, Almost three-in-ten citizens globally say they have started a business at some point. July 22, 2022.

Silicon Valley, there is a Canadian 'mafia,'" referring to the various CEOs, CTOs, and CIOs of U.S. technology companies who are Canadian and are thriving outside the country. "In Canada, these Canadians didn't find the environment for which they could do what they have done."

Broadcaster and author Amanda Lang brought up another aspect of the increasingly complex relationship between Canada and the United States. "The double-edged sword that we now hold in our hands is we are perfectly positioned to attract the expansion of multinationals, especially big US companies. We've already seen Google, Facebook, and Amazon look north." They look north because of the stability, similarities, lower Canadian dollar, and ease of movement of material and employees. "The downside of that," Lang said, "is our human capital goes to foreign multinationals. So Google takes our best talent, and in the end the product of their labour and the fruit of their education and everything we've invested in them winds up going to a publicly traded American firm."

Is this a good or a bad thing? "People will debate violently whether it's a problem or not," Lang said. "But you could see how it could be a problem." It would essentially perpetuate the branch plant economy that has plagued Canada's economic partnership with the United States. "But maybe better to have those players even though they're going to steal our best talent because there's so much spillover benefit."

Canada has a few things going for it in the technology space. It does have a vibrant start-up scene that is producing hundreds of technology companies every year. Canada is seen as a global leader in artificial intelligence. Toronto is growing technology jobs faster than any other city in North America. The Canadian technology sector is undergoing a mini technology boom, and Toronto's tech work force is also growing quicker than any U.S. hub.[27]

And during the Trump presidency, the United States lost some of its lustre as the top destination for technology jobs. Technology professionals looked elsewhere, including Canada which benefitted enormously from its ability to bring in skilled workers from around the world.[28]

"It certainly seems that talented people are having trouble getting to the United States and looking at Canada instead," said Steve Mayer, president and managing director of Greenhill Canada. "This could work to our benefit. Canada needs to be smart to capture those people and make sure the conditions are as favorable as possible, so that entrepreneurs and innovators who come to this market are able to thrive."

While Canada had a small window to attract talent, it has struggled to be a go-to destination for global technology professionals.

Adam Froman, founder and CEO of Delvinia, notes that many Canadian universities are really focused on the foreign multinationals, not Canadian scaleups. "But most of us need experienced talent," he said. "I don't think we've had a strong effort to attract people to move to Canada from India or from eastern European countries. There is definitely a huge opportunity for that."

This isn't to say that Canadians aren't at all innovative. It is worth looking at the success of Canada's Technology Triangle—the cities of Waterloo, Kitchener, and Cambridge, to see how that success was

27 See https://www.nytimes.com/2022/03/21/technology/toronto-tech-boom.html
28 See https://www.businessinsider.com/toronto-canada-tech-hub-immigrants-h1b-visa-2020-7

achieved. In 2007, Waterloo, with a modest population of 120,000 was named Intelligent Community of the Year by the Intelligent Community Forum,[29] which cited the region's 334 technology companies (now more than 1,570 tech-related businesses), its post-secondary institutions (University of Waterloo, Wilfrid Laurier University, Conestoga College), and perhaps most importantly, the cooperation between business and academia.

The evolution of the Waterloo region followed a familiar North American pattern, starting as an agricultural community, then becoming an industrial base. It saw rapid expansion (in 1965, Kitchener was the fastest-growing city in Canada), and then the industries died. It started with grist mills, then tanneries, breweries, and shoe factories. It was once the Button Capital and then the Rubber Capital. But manufacturing was lost to offshore operations, and, as a result, the local factories closed. America's rust belt is littered with stories like this.

What set Waterloo apart were two things: a curious combination of entrepreneurial spirit and conservatism and the rise of the University of Waterloo (UW). The UW was established in 1957 by two local businessmen. One was Gerry Hagey, a PR man for the B.F. Goodrich tire company, who became the university's first president. The initial focus of the university was to turn out engineers and actuaries for the local insurance companies. Hagey implemented a co-op program where engineering students were in the workforce for four months of the year. This idea was ridiculed by other Canadian universities. At the

29 Waterloo named the World's Top Intelligent Community, Centre for International Governance. March 18, 2007. https://www.cigionline.org/articles/waterloo-named-worlds-top-intelligent-community/

time there was a pronounced divide between academia and industry, and most universities wanted to keep it that way. It was the era of the Ivory Tower.[30]

Mathematics was a key part of the UW curriculum, which also made it unique. In 1960, it was usually studied by people who loved the discipline; there wasn't much in the way of practical application. But the head of the math department, Ralph Stanton, realized that it was a field that would become increasingly important. In 1960, UW established its Computer Centre, and suddenly math had a practical purpose. It expanded quickly and in 1967, became the first computer faculty at any North American university.

At the time, computers were still larger than cars, and sat in heavily cooled rooms, out of sight. The Computer Centre was run by Wes Graham, who allowed undergraduates to use the computers, a radical notion at the time. IBM credited him with democratizing what was then an elitist world. Given access to the computers, the students designed early computer languages (WATFOR and WATFIV). Graham formed a campus group to distribute the software and it evolved into Watcom, the first computing company to come out of the university. This was a great example of giving people the proper tools and getting rewarded for it.

By 1984, UW had one of the world's largest computing programs and it continued its alliance with local business through its co-op program. It also allowed students to retain the intellectual rights to anything they developed. The result was that UW spawned more than 250 science and tech companies, including Open Text, which turned

30 Don Gillmor, The invention of Waterloo. *The Walrus*, 9(1), pp.44-49, 2012. https://thewalrus.ca/the-invention-of-waterloo/.

out to be one of the most important, going on to become Canada's largest software company. It got the contract to digitize the Oxford English Dictionary. At the time, few thought it was a worthwhile project, but the technologies they developed for that project were later adapted by Yahoo! Technology is like Wayne Gretzky's view of hockey: you don't skate to where the puck is, but where it's going.

Perhaps the most important company to come out of UW was Research in Motion (Blackberry). Mike Lazaridis was a UW engineering student who left the programme to start his own business with the tacit support of the dean. RIM grew into a multi-billion-dollar company, creating more than 7,000 jobs in the area. As the RIM founders grew wealthy, they contributed hundreds of millions of dollars to the area, reinforcing it as a hub for intellectual capital and research. Lazaridis used $170 million to found the Perimeter Institute for Theoretical Physics. In 2002, he followed it up by establishing the Institute for Quantum Computing. Lazaridis said that the Blackberry was essentially based on 19th-century physics. "Imagine what we could do with twentieth-century physics or twenty-first century physics."

There are many incredible Canadian successes, stories that showcase how Canadians have achieved innovative successes. A smart book by David Johnston and Tom Jenkins entitled *Innovation Nation: How Canadian Innovators Made the World Smarter, Smaller, Kinder, Safer, Healthier, Wealthier, Happier* was released on Canada's 150th birthday. The book is meant to "celebrate the history and spirit of creativity in Canada." The innovations are listed in the table below.

Category	Invention
Smarter	Duck Decoy, Light Bulb, Electric Radio, Dump Truck, Snow Science, Blackberry
Smaller	Canoe, Toboggan, Telephone, Snowmobile, Walkie-Talkie, Canadarm, Java
Kinder	Longhouse, Forensic Pathology, Declaration of Human Rights, Garbage Bag, Electric Wheelchair, Blue Box Recycling, Right to Play
Safer	Igloo, Life Jacket, Foghorn, Roberson Screwdriver, Gas Mask, Shrouded Tuyere, Goalie Mask
Healthier	Peanut Butter, Buckley's Mixture, Insulin, Atlas of the Heart, Prosthetic Hand, Sulcabrush, Telesurgery
Wealthier	Canada Dry, Chocolate Bar, Whoopee Cushion, Shreddies, Instant Replay, Digital Photography, IMAX
Happier	Maple Syrup, Lacrosse, McIntosh Apple, Hockey, Basketball, Zipper, Superman, Cirque du Soleil, Internet Search Engine

Source: David Johnston and Tom Jenkins, 2017. *Innovation Nation: How Canadian Innovators Made the World Smarter, Smaller, Kinder, Safer, Healthier, Wealthier, Happier.*

In order to innovate, you need innovative people. Canada has one of the highest immigration rates in the world, but we don't always attract the most innovative people. One of the reasons is the country's tax rates, which are not attractive for ambitious global entrepreneurs. William B.P. Robson argues that Canada needs to keep its top personal tax rate below 50 percent. It is currently 53.5 percent. "It's a psychologically significant level," he said, "and if it's psychologically significant, it's economically significant," Robson said.

The Canadian government has introduced initiatives to encourage coding, and in 2017 it invested $50 million to equip youth with digital skills. In its first two years, CanCode reached more than 1.3 million students and more than 61,000 teachers. Abdullah Snobar, executive director of the DMZ tech accelerator at Toronto Metropolitan University, said that schools need to have technology-related education focusing on areas around Science, Technology, Engineering and Mathematics (STEM), starting off at the youngest age, and coding should be mandatory. After years of slipping in its global educational rankings, Canada cracked the top ten for math, science, and reading, taking its place with the world's leading educational powerhouses in Asia and Europe (OECD, PISA, 2016).[31] But this success should not limit further improvements in Canada's educational curriculum, as there are many remaining gaps.

In addition to Canada's historic reliance on resources to underpin our past prosperity, the country has always benefitted from access to the U.S. market ready to consume a large share of Canadian exports. However, the rise of U.S. protectionism under President Trump demonstrated that relying so heavily on such a strategy is unwise. Canadians must develop export markets well beyond the United States, and reach into fast-growing emerging markets. In order to succeed in increasingly competitive global markets, Canadian firms must improve their productivity and innovation capacities. Opening more foreign markets is essential to diversify Canadian trade, but not sufficient.

Canadian governments must remove the implicit policy biases that discourage the global diversification of the Canadian economy. There are costly implications to remaining complacent. Many of the basic services Canadians take for granted—such as health care

---

31 OECD, PISA, Programme for International Student Assessment. 2016. https://
www.oecd.org/pisa/

and education—will come under increasing threat as the economy weakens and government tax revenue dwindles. It is also important to keep in mind that education and health care are not charity but investments in people, because a productive Canadian must be healthy and educated to work and fully contribute to the economy. The rising government and personal debt levels and resulting pressures could threaten the inclusive fabric and diverse identity of Canada. In a depressed economy, citizens could look for a scapegoat. We need to recognize the urgency of the situation and to effect change. Change that is implemented proactively is almost always more successful than reactive change. We can't wait for negative events to drive us to action and as we look ahead we must recognize, "[i]t is time to bring people together as we hopefully move beyond the negative events of the pandemic and chart a path forward to strengthen the economy, create jobs, and promote confidence in a shared future," said Goldy Hyder, CEO of the Business Council of Canada.

In our wide consultations and interviews for this book, the most cited reason for Canada's underperformance is culture. It is argued that Canadians are risk averse and there is an almost irredeemable stigma associated with failure. And hence the reluctance to undertake entrepreneurial endeavours that may lead to failure.

"It has a lot to do with everybody protecting their own. We are slow to change in Canada," said Annette Verschuren. "We have the elements of the greatest country in the world. (But) I do think we are behind on externalities. As a country, we are risk-averse. Some businesses are easy to start in Canada, but many are very difficult, especially those in industries that are heavily protected. We are not good to the people who take risks here. We don't celebrate them."

There is a need to shine a spotlight on individuals and companies that make it. "In Canada, we don't embrace successful entrepreneurs the same way that they become celebrities in the U.S. Part of that is our culture, which is to be a little more modest and not thump your chest as much," said Steve Mayer, President and Managing Director of Greenhill Canada. "We need to celebrate successes and hold out those examples, so that they inspire a new generation of entrepreneurs."

The 2009 Survey of Innovation and Business Strategy undertaken by Industry Canada[32] reports that "risk and uncertainty was the greatest obstacle noted by business owners when asked about what it was that was keeping them from investing in growth through innovation. In addition, Canadian business owners' aversion to risk transcends all industries and grows along with company size."[33]

There is significant disagreement over whether this risk aversion is the result of Canadian culture at the individual level, or the result of conservative Canadian institutions and government policy.

At a panel discussion on this topic at the Rotman School of Management that included the authors Assaf and Hejazi, both former Dean, Roger Martin and former Governor of the Bank of Canada, Mark Carney, argued that it was not culture, but rather economic incentives that explain the differences. The interviews conducted for this book support this view; many of those interviewed expressed their frustration in pursuing entrepreneurial endeavours within Canada.

---

32 Industry Canada, Survey of Innovation and Business Strategy (SIBS). https://www.ic.gc.ca/eic/site/eas-aes.nsf/eng/h_ra02092.html

33 Don Ovsey, Are fat and happy Canadians too chicken to invest in growth and innovation? *Financial Post*, October 1, 2012. https://business.financialpost.com/executive/are-fat-and-happy-canadians-too-chicken-to-invest-in-growth-and-innovation

Furthermore, some of the issues and challenges facing Canada that arose in our interviews were also discussed in two important studies by Roger Martin.[34, 35]

Brandon A. Lee, Consul General of Canada in Seattle, said that there was a difference in the way the Silicon Valley culture worked. "In Silicon Valley," he said, "for many tech companies, the default idea is yes, and you have to write a business case if you want to say no. That's how they embrace innovation. So in that way, as you know, many areas of Canada maybe are a little more conservative, right? And innovation is slow, especially in larger companies."

Richard Osborn, managing partner at Telus Ventures, characterized the difference between Canadian and U.S. investors. "The way I would describe the difference is a Canadian person with capital wakes up and thinks, 'dear God, don't let me lose it'. The American guy wakes up and goes, 'dear God, don't let me miss out on a good deal.'" This view was reinforced by Tony Lacavera, who argued that there is an aspiration gap between Canadians and Americans: "In the U.S. meetings, start-ups are thinking of the global domination. In the Canadian meetings, it's all about mitigating the downside."[36]

Canadian conservatism has worked well in the past, but it will work against Canada in the future. Our investment in new technologies is too small.

34 Martin, R.L. and Milway, J., 2012. Canada: What it Is, what it Can be. University of Toronto Press.

35 Martin, R.L. and Porter, M.E., 2001. Canadian competitiveness: A decade after the crossroads. CD Howe Institute).

36 Book Launch, Wednesday November 1, 2017. Rotman School of Management. Anthony Lacavera and Kate Fillion, How we can win: and what happens to us and our country if we don't hardcover. October 3, 2017.

Canadian complacency may also be a function of history, with our economy being initially tightly connected with the United Kingdom, then the world's largest economy, and supplanted by the United States, the world's subsequent largest economy. Sharing a language, history, and similar culture made trade with the United Kingdom and the United States seems easy, and as a result Canadians don't have experience at building trade relationships and properly benchmarking risk when such similarities don't exist. The good news is that Canadian complacency seems culturally situational and not dispositional, and we can be retrained with the right mindset and mentorship.

The issues around innovation are exemplified through the experiences of Dr. Waqaas Al-Siddiq, the thirty-six-year-old founder, Chairman, President, and CEO of Biotricity, a medtech start-up. Al-Siddiq grew up in Winnipeg, a gifted student who went from grade eight to university, going through puberty while earning an engineering degree (which could be a chapter on its own). When he was 14, his family moved to Seattle, so he had a taste of the two cultures. He had a master's degree by 19 and worked at IBM and other tech companies before starting his own. "I was always interested in health care," he said. "I always felt the future was in remote diagnostic monitoring and so went on my own to launch this thing."

He developed a device that monitors cardiac health, the largest health market; heart disease is the number one cause of death in the United States. "It was a diagnostic device that collects patients' ECG in real time and analyzes it," he said, "and when it determines there is an emergency, it transmits that to a call centre, and they review the data and get the patient into the hospital or into the cardiologist."

Al-Siddiq had done some of his university education in Toronto and he looked for his initial funding there. But health care start-ups pose particular challenges. "First you go through all the regulation," he said, "so you have to convince them it is effective, safe, and clinically relevant. But that doesn't mean you can commercialize it. Now you have the healthcare payer to go through. Who's going to pay?" Al-Siddiq began with the business model. "I figured out the commercialization first. I don't want to look at any product without understanding the whole path of commercialization."

The problem was that there wasn't a clear path to commercialization in Canada. Our health care system has much to commend, and in most ways, is much better than the U.S. model. The private American system has many drawbacks, but it does reward innovation. In Canada, Al-Siddiq said, "it will cost doctors more to deploy my technology. We are safer and better for the patient, unfortunately maybe five to ten percent of doctors care about that. For most of them it's about the bottom line."

While he found his initial funding in Canada, he quickly hit a wall and had to look elsewhere. In the end, he found the money in New York and found his employees in California. Biotricity is now listed on the Nasdaq exchange and has delivered consistent quarter-over-quarter gains. Why did this company go to the United States?

"If you're an entrepreneur developing technology and setting up a business in Canada and you have any experience in the US, it's a no-brainer," he said. One reason to set up in the United States is the size and nature of venture capital in the two countries. Understandably, there is more in the United States, but it isn't just the quantity but the quality. Canadian investors want an early, steady return; they are looking for immediate profitability. But profitability comes at the expense of growth. "If you chase profitability," he said, "now you're an M&A play and you're never going to grow."

Another issue is productivity and the culture in Silicon Valley. "In California, they know it's a race," Al-Siddiq said, "and they want to out-produce, and the only way to do that is put in more hours and more time. To find talent that is just willing to outwork everybody else is much easier in the United States. You pay more for them, but they make up for that in productivity. It's all about productivity and they are way more productive. California is an accelerant. I can accelerate my product and my development lifecycle."

The medtech device he developed is now used by 1,500 cardiologists across 23 states. "We literally save lives every day," Al-Siddiq said, "because there are patients, that if they weren't on our monitor, they would either never wake up, or they would end up in the ER with a massive stroke or heart attack that would be debilitating." It is a device that saves lives, but just as importantly in a capitalist system, it saves money.

He has expanded to other countries, but Canada may not see his device. The health system is under provincial jurisdiction, meaning several small markets, several bureaucracies and political regimes. "I have to think about ROI (return on investment) and if I go into Alberta, for example, what's my cost to go into that market? What's my ROI on those dollars? From a business perspective, it makes no sense. There are so many better places for me to spend those dollars, and this is the problem."

This is a big problem, one that got bigger during the pandemic. Increasingly, the ability to innovate is critical in the medical world. COVID-19 brought out the best in many individuals but the worst in our system.

The COVID-19 pandemic brought tremendous financial hardship to those in certain industries. Travel, restaurants, and retail all suffered.

A third of Canadian businesses lost at least 40 percent of their revenue. Another 20 percent lost at least 20 percent.[37] More than two million jobs were lost in Canada in April 2020, a record.[38] But the pandemic also brought out an entrepreneurial spirit. People came up with ingenious ways to create distanced outdoor dining experiences, to deliver anything and everything, to adapt to the market.

The other thing COVID-19 did was to accelerate the pace of e-commerce dramatically. Shopify, which was at one point Canada's largest company by market capitalization, went into the capital markets to raise $1.55 billion in February 2021. "Why the raise?" asked Katie Keita, Shopify's senior director. "Well, 2020 effectively fast-forwarded commerce five years into the future. In this new reality where the centre of gravity is digital, we need to accelerate our investment plans. Raising capital strengthens our balance sheet to provide more flexibility to be more opportunistic to build, partner and potentially acquire."[39]

The COVID-19 crisis also revealed the disadvantages to a risk-averse culture. By not developing our own vaccines or making a bet on our own version of the American Warp Speed strategy, we relied on other countries to provide us with them. Understandably, their priority was to vaccinate their own citizens. As a result, our vaccination rates lagged.

37 Pete Evans, More than 50% of Canadian companies have lost at least one-fifth of their revenue to COVID-19, StatsCan says. CBC News. April 29, 2020.
38 Statistics Canada, Labour Force Survey, April 2020. https://www150.statcan.gc.ca/n1/daily-quotidien/200508/dq200508a-eng.htm
39 Sean Silcoff, Shopify taps frenzied market for third time in a year, raising US$1.55-billion in stock offering. *The Globe and Mail*, February 23, 2021. https://www.theglobeandmail.com/business/article-shopify-again-taps-frenzied-market-for-third-time-in-a-year-raising/

In the *Globe and Mail,* medical columnist Andre Picard took stock of the full year after Canada recorded its first COVID-19 death, on March 8, 2020. "First of all," he wrote, "we've learned when alarm bells go off, Canadian politicians and health officials don't exactly spring into action. They express condolences, they fidget, they ponder—but they are reluctant to act quickly and forcefully."[40]

While provinces declared a state of emergency, lockdowns weren't implemented. We were reactive, rather than proactive. While Canada's infection rates were initially a fraction of the United States, there were repercussions to the slow action taken by Canadian politicians. Toronto has had some of the longest business closures of any other city in North America, with devastating results.[41] As Picard pointed out, we failed to learn from our mistakes; the first wave was deadly, the second wave was worse.

John Lewis, a biotechnology executive, told parliament that the funding wasn't sufficient to develop vaccines. The National Research Council of Canada distributed $23 million to vaccine developers, with no one getting more than $5 million. By comparison, Britain gave AstraZeneca hundreds of millions to develop a vaccine. The Canadian federal government "took a careful, risk-averse and committee-based decision approach that led to a relatively modest amount of scattered funding for companies in Canada to develop domestic vaccines," Lewis said. The results were underwhelming. At any rate, Canada has limited capabilities to mass-produce a vaccine. "Expecting other

40 André Picard, A year of pandemic death ends with some rays of hope. *The Globe and Mail,* March 9, 2021. https://www.theglobeandmail.com/opinion/article-a-year-of-pandemic-death-ends-with-some-rays-of-hope/

41 Robin Levinson-King, Toronto lockdown—one of the world's longest? BBC News Online, May 24, 2021. https://www.bbc.com/news/world-us-canada-57079577

countries to develop and manufacture vaccines and not prioritize their own population was, I think, a little misguided," Lewis said.[42]

Developing a vaccine required significant up-front investments on the part of governments. That investment is fraught with risk. What if the vaccine isn't successful? What if it arrives too late? But the safe, risk-averse route can have dire consequences as well. Unfortunately, the consequences for Canada become more apparent as many of the world's economies opened more quickly, while we remained in the starting blocks.

If Canada's innovation scorecard doesn't improve, citizens will continue to suffer economically and potentially socially, as Canadian GDP and personal incomes fall further behind that of our trading partners. This trend will have deleterious effects on the government's ability to provide social programmes, and Canada's very fabric as an inclusive and tolerant country will come under strain.

Complacency has plagued Canadian administrations of all stripes—both Liberal and Conservative. It is often the case that change is not implemented until economic conditions and prosperity deteriorate significantly. As Canada falls further behind our trading partners both in terms of GDP and GDP per capita, the case for change becomes stronger and stronger.

Armuhghan Ahmad , President & Managing Partner, Digital at KPMG, shared these thoughts, "The future economy of Canada relies on innovation to drive growth and prosperity for all citizens. To sustain current growth of the innovation economy, growing at three to six times faster than the traditional parts of the economy, we need to learn

---

42 Open Parliament. Testimony before Parliamentary Health Committee. February 22, 2021. https://openparliament.ca/search/?q=Witness%3A+%22271842%22

from our experiences during the pandemic that brought on the Great Resignation to foster a better work and life balance. Looking forward we need a Great Realignment of our priorities to build a purpose-driven economy that unlocks our individual creativity and entrepreneurial spirit driven by an era fueled by a growth mindset and exponential leadership."

This book is a call to action to begin the change needed to reverse these trends immediately. Being proactive in effecting change also delivers better results than a reactive and risk-averse perspective. We need to become more excited at the prospect of winning innovation races than hesitant due to the fear of losing. Canada needs bold leadership and the input of all Canadians to ensure it continues to live up to the promise of Canada.

3

Bracing for Future Shocks: Canada in Historical Economic Contexts

I am not afraid of storms, for I am learning how to sail my ship.
—Louisa May Alcott

The year 1967 has a special resonance for Canadians. It was the country's centennial, and millions from around the world came to celebrate at Montreal's Expo 67. Canada was ranked the world's 9th largest economy. But other economies have since surpassed us. By 2017, we had fallen to 16th and projections for the next fifty years indicate this trend will continue. Based on our extensive analysis, Canada's rank can be expected to fall to 25th place by 2067. The following countries are expected to top Canada in economic size: Indonesia, Mexico, Brazil, Nigeria, Pakistan, Egypt, Turkey, Saudi Arabia, Vietnam, the Philippines, Bangladesh, Iran, Malaysia, and Thailand.

"Ultimately the weight of a country in the world is going to depend on its economic power and its military power. Canada has slipped in both categories," said William B.P. Robson, president and CEO of the C.D. Howe Institute. To understand Canada's economy in broader historical context, it is helpful to look at historic powers such as the United States, the former Soviet Union, and China.

The Sliding Importance of the United States

While the United States hasn't lost much ground from a military perspective, globally it has lost ground economically. When President Joe Biden announced his infrastructure plan on March 31, 2021, he acknowledged that America was headed in the wrong direction. His multi-trillion-dollar proposal was the boldest in more than a generation. There was, Biden said, a need to be bold. His predecessor, Donald Trump, had looked to the past to comfort America, first to the 1950s, when the United States was the only legitimate superpower, then to the 1930s and the protectionist tariffs of the Smoot–Hawley Act, and finally to the 19th century, with his championing of coal. Meanwhile, the rest of the world was moving into the future. China, Biden noted, "is eating our lunch."[43] Japan and Europe were aggressively embracing the future.

You could have substituted "Canada" for the word "America" and his speech would have resonated almost equally. For both countries, a dangerous complacency had set in. Biden's Secretary of Transportation, Pete Buttegieg, noted that America ranked 13th in the world in terms

---

43 Amanda Macias, Biden warns China is going to "eat our lunch" if U.S. doesn't get moving on infrastructure. CNBC, February 11, 2021. https://www.cnbc.com/2021/02/11/biden-says-china-will-eat-our-lunch-on-infrastructure.html

of its infrastructure.[44] It was once number one. He pointed out that broadband was as critical a part of infrastructure as roads and bridges, but that 35 percent of rural Americans lacked access to high-speed internet. He promised that every single American would have access to high-speed, high-quality internet.[45] "Americans pay too much for internet service," he said. However, they pay far less than Canadians.

Included in the Infrastructure bill were provisions for a pivot away from fossil fuels. No country has celebrated fossil fuels the way the United States has. It was the source of some of the country's largest fortunes (Rockefeller's Standard Oil), it underpinned the economy and swagger of Texas and other states, and it fuelled the great American romance with the automobile and the open road. American gas prices were among the lowest in the developed world. So it isn't just an environmental pivot but a cultural pivot. It's fine to nostalgically remember driving on an uncluttered road in a 1963 Cadillac that got 14 miles to the gallon. But there are dangers to trying to live in the past, as Trump's presidency demonstrated.

Tom Steyer, a billionaire activist who advised the Biden administration on climate change, said, "This is an opportunity to equitably shape America's future prosperity and role in the world. It's time to think big and get it done."[46]

---

44 These rankings are provided by the World Economic Forum, The Global Competitiveness Report 2019. https://www3.weforum.org/docs/WEF_TheGlobalCompetitivenessReport2019.pdf

45 See https://ca.finance.yahoo.com/news/gina-raimondo-rural-broadband-access-193142826.html

46 Steven Mufson and Juliet Eilperin, Biden's infrastructure plan aims to turbocharge U.S. shift from fossil fuels. *The Washington Post*, March 31, 2021. https://www.washingtonpost.com/climate-environment/2021/03/31/biden-climate-infrastructure/

Biden's proposals included $174 billion to the American share of electric vehicles, establishing 500,000 electric vehicle charging stations, and $35 billion to develop cutting-edge technologies to combat climate change. During Trump's presidency, America lost its role as a global leader, and nature abhors a vacuum; China and others were happy to step in. The world made great strides at America's expense.

Biden promised the "most innovative economy in the world." At that moment, it was no longer the most innovative economy. And there are reasons for that. Biden pointed out that the United States was one of the few developed nations whose investment in research and development had declined over the past twenty-five years. Decades ago, it was 2 percent; in 2020 it was 1.7 percent.

Almost everything Biden said about America losing its place in the world would apply to Canada. Drastic steps needed to be taken. "We've fallen back," he said. "The rest of the world is closing in and closing fast." In many areas, the world had already surpassed America. The United States ranked 27th in terms of health care (down from 6th in 1990); 17th in education (though 38th in math, and 24th in science); it was 43rd in life expectancy, though a health forecasting study from the Institute for Health Metrics and Evaluation predicted it would slide to 64th by 2040.[47] One of the few areas it ranked highly was gun-related deaths, where it was number two (behind Brazil). It wasn't in Biden's political interests to specifically point out how

---

47 See https://www.usatoday.com/story/news/nation-now/2018/10/18/u-s-life-expectancy-forecast-take-plunge-2040-study-finds/1680848002/ and https://www.healthdata.org/news-release/how-healthy-will-we-be-2040. See also https://www.thelancet.com/journals/lancet/article/PIIS0140-6736(18)31694-5/fulltext#seccestitle160

far the country had fallen; America's mythology relies on it being the Greatest Nation on Earth, a phrase that is repeated every four years during presidential elections. And while there is much that is great about the United States, like Canada, it has failed to keep pace with the change that was happening so quickly in the rest of the world. Even our mighty neighbour, a country that had once created the future, seemed in danger of being left behind.

The Collapse of the Soviet Union

In 1967, there were two military superpowers: the Soviet Union and the United States. In 1991, the Soviet Union collapsed, resulting in economic and political reverberations across the world, and left a single superpower. In the aftermath of this collapse, fourteen states achieved their independence: Armenia, Azerbaijan, Belarus, Estonia, Georgia, Kazakhstan, Kyrgyzstan, Latvia, Lithuania, Moldova, Tajikistan, Turkmenistan, Ukraine, and Uzbekistan. The movement away from Communism, which had stifled people's creativity and potential, led to a system where Inga in Lithuania could pursue her passion for shoes, and where Estonia became a hub for innovative start-ups. Entrepreneurship and businesses flourished, and many of these countries experienced greater economic growth as they joined the rest of the free market world. As a group, these former Soviet economies have experienced higher economic growth rates than Canada. Table 1 benchmarks Canada's growth performance against these former Soviet states, the United Kingdom, the United States, Germany, Japan, China and India.

Table 1 Real GDP Growth, Former States within the Soviet Union

	1990s	2000s	2010–2019	2020	2021–2025
Former States of the Soviet Union	-1.2%	7.4%	4.2%	-3.7%	4.1%
Canada	2.4%	2.1%	2.2%	-7.1%	2.9%
United Kingdom	2.2%	1.8%	1.9%	-9.8%	2.9%
United States	3.2%	1.9%	2.3%	-4.3%	2.4%
Germany	2.2%	0.8%	1.9%	-6.0%	2.3%
Japan	1.5%	0.5%	1.3%	-5.3%	1.3%
China	10.0%	10.4%	7.7%	1.9%	6.2%
India	5.7%	6.9%	7.0%	-10.3%	7.8%

Data source: International Monetary Fund.

Note: Former States of the Soviet Union include Armenia, Azerbaijan, Belarus, Estonia, Georgia, Kazakhstan, Kyrgyzstan, Latvia, Lithuania, Moldova, Tajikistan, Turkmenistan, Ukraine, and Uzbekistan.

China's Emergence from Isolation

In 1967 China was an inward-looking, isolated economy and one of the poorest countries in the world on a per-capita basis. The 1978 Chinese Communist Party reforms under Deng Xiaoping began China's re-emergence as a global powerhouse, allowing it access to Western markets and technology and wealth. Along with massive investments in infrastructure, the Chinese economy experienced spectacular growth. Almost 800 million people in China were lifted out of poverty.[48] Today, on a Purchasing Power Parity (PPP)

48 See https://www.worldbank.org/en/news/press-release/2022/04/01/lifting-800-million-people-out-of-poverty-new-report-looks-at-lessons-from-china-s-experience

basis, China is the largest economy in the world, as it was 200 years ago.[49]

China was once viewed as an economy that only produced low-cost goods for export. This changed as China rapidly moved up the value chain in the same way Japan and South Korea had done. Fifty years ago, Japan and South Korea sold cheap goods to the world, using imported and copied technology. These countries now supply the world with some of the most technologically advanced products. This same pattern is being mirrored in China. The global landscape has changed in ways unimaginable only decades ago.

Consider the emergence of machine learning and artificial intelligence—the idea that computers have the ability to make cognitive decisions and learn from human behaviours. This area is advancing at breakneck speed. As expected, technology giants such as Google, Amazon, and Apple are leading the charge. However, according to an article by Professors Avi Goldfarb and Daniel Trefler, "China is becoming an AI superpower faster than most of the world has anticipated — so much so, it's poised to match Silicon Valley's authority in the tech arena."[50]

China's transformation from an agricultural society to an advanced manufacturing economy happened in just five decades. While China is the world's largest economy on a PPP basis, its income per person is only 20 percent of that of the United States. China's growth over this period was driven in part by opening the economy to trade and investment, along with reforms instituted in the 1970s. A key component of that

---

49 Angus Maddison, *The World Economy: Volume 1: A Millennial Perspective and Volume 2.* Historical Statistics Development Centre of the OECD, 2006. P. 263.

50 Darah Hansen. China poised to take lead in artificial intelligence race. *The Globe and Mail*, May 18, 2018. https://tgam.ca/33KPz9x

growth involved "internal immigration/urbanisation"—the exodus of tens of millions of people from the countryside to the cities. China grew aggressively, mainly through this reallocation of labour from low-productivity agricultural activities in the countryside to more productive manufacturing opportunities in cities. As China's economy matured in the post-2010 period, its pace of growth has slowed dramatically, wages have naturally increased, and the Chinese currency has appreciated. This resulted in the erosion of its competitiveness and reliance on low costs for production, which has accelerated because of its trade war with the United States. Much of the low-cost production is no longer in China, destined for other Asian countries with lower costs, such as Bangladesh, Cambodia, Vietnam, Thailand, and others.[51]

In this regard, China and Canada have a lot in common. Both economies are at an inflexion point. China must continue to transform itself away from being a low-cost mass producer of goods, relying on copied and imported technology and diversify away from the U.S. economy. In other words, a strategy that delivered much of the growth and prosperity over the past fifty years will not guarantee success going forward. China's economy must evolve, moving away from a model of replication, low-value and high-volume product mixes towards creating new technologies and world-class products.

The story of Jack Ma and Ant Group suggests that China will only go so far when it comes to innovation and free market philosophy. Ma created China's largest and most innovative fintech conglomerate, a source of pride for the country. But he publicly criticized China's regulators for being too cautious, suggesting that they needed to

---

51 See: https://www.usnews.com/news/best-countries/slideshows/countries-seen-to-have-the-lowest-manufacturing-costs

expand their lending criteria to fuel innovation. The government wasn't amused, and blocked Ant Group's IPO, which was expected to be $34 billion, one of the largest ever.[52] When economic power and market dynamics are subservient to political will, over time, it will erode innovation and economic growth. This trend is expected to continue in China with Xi Jinping's tighter grip on power. "A central committee, politburo and standing committee dominated by Xi would mean a significant loss of checks and balances. Xi's policy of putting ideology and national security over economic development will continue for the coming five or even 10 years as he is eager to rule until the 22nd party congress in 2032 when he will be 79." Citation: Willy Lam, a senior fellow at Jamestown Foundation, a Washington-based thinktank, as cited in the Guardian (https://www.theguardian.com/world/2022/oct/22/xi-jinping-tightens-grip-on-power-as-chinas-communist-party-elevates-his-status?CMP=oth_b-aplnews_d-1) Markets ultimately serve consumers, not politicians, and foreigners are becoming less trusting and increasingly scared to invest in China by the government's mercurial efforts to control the market. And it's not just foreigners that are worried. Fears among China's wealthy have increased after "a series of temporary or longer-term disappearances of high-profile people from public view over recent years, including Alibaba founder Jack Ma, tennis star Peng Shuai, elite financier Xiao Jianhua and real estate mogul Whitney Duan." As a result, many are fleeing China, or at least ready to do so. "The family motto has always been: 'Keep a fast junk in the harbour with gold bars and a second set of papers'. The modern

---

52 Raymond Zhong, In halting Ant's I.P.O., China sends a warning to business. *New York Times*, December 24, 2020. https://www.nytimes.com/2020/11/06/technology/china-ant-group-ipo.html

equivalent would be a private jet, a couple of passports and foreign bank accounts," Lesperance says. "That is the world we are in . . . it is tough stuff."[53] One important index ranks China's capital accounts openness at 106th.[54]

Faith in Chinese leadership was further eroded during the punitive lockdowns, a futile attempt to bring COVID-19 numbers to zero. Frustrated citizens investigated online forums titled "run xue"—run philosophy, code for emigration, which spiked.

Like developed countries found in the post–Second World War period, China should allow for greater foreign investment and continue to open up its industries to reach its full potential. This benefitted its economy, as well as satisfied global demands for reciprocity in Chinese investment policy. The Chinese government enacted policies to transform its economy and embrace the industries of the future, and protections for intellectual property improved significantly.[55] However, the failure of China to open its economy further carries great risk to its economic future. A card game that only benefits the dealer will not have many players at its table.

China has also been aggressive in pursuing green energy solutions. For the Chinese, the issue is existential. One study estimated that a third of the country's deaths were related to smog.[56] Many are familiar with

53 China's wealthy activate escape plans as Xi Jinping extends rule. *Financial Times*, October 24 2022 https://on.ft.com/3U0JmQj.

54 See Why China is not rising as a financial superpower, *Financial Times*, June 20, 2022 by Ruchir Sharma. https://www.ft.com/content/233b101e-7d51-11e9-81d2-f785092ab560

55 Walid Hejazi, Sarah Kutulakos, and Daniela Stratulativ, Canada-China Business Survey 2020/2021, Canada China Business Council. https://ccbc.com/wp-content/uploads/2021/10/2020-2021-Busines_Survey-Report.pdf

56 Alice Yan, Smog linked to third of deaths in China, study finds. *South China*

images of Beijing where it looks like it's enveloped in coal dust, where visibility is a few metres. And, as of this writing, Beijing isn't among the top ten polluted Chinese cities (it weighs in at number eleven).

According to the International Renewable Energy Agency, there are almost ten times more people in China working in the solar power sector than in the United States: 2.5 million versus 260,000.[57] The country is investing extensively in automation and renewable energy. China is aggressively positioning its economy for the future.

As both a customer and a competitor, Canada needs to strike that balance and have a plan to deal with China's growing influence. The West requires "a positive, offensive strategy to compete with China," RiceHadleyGates principal Anja Manuel wrote in a *Financial Times* piece.[58] She advocates for a "Tech 10" group of countries that "set global ethical standards for artificial intelligence and digital privacy; and worked on norms for biotech to prevent dangerous gene-editing experiments on humans."

Economic revival has not been limited to the former Soviet States and China over the past fifty years. India has continued to advance rapidly (although divisive political rhetoric is rising there too creating social tensions), while Brazil and South Africa have shown choppy growth. Bloomberg listed the world's twenty most attractive emerging markets in 2018 based on growth rates, yields, trade balances, and

Morning Post, December 22, 2016. https://www.scmp.com/news/china/society/article/2056553/smog-linked-third-deaths-china-study-finds

57 Sherisse Pham and Matt Rivers, China is crushing the U.S. in renewable energy. *CNN Business,* July 18, 2017. https://money.cnn.com/2017/07/18/technology/china-us-clean-energy-solar-farm/index.html

58 Anja Manuel, The West needs a positive response to China's technology challenge. *Financial Times,* August 14, 2019. https://on.ft.com/33GDHWf

asset valuations as: Mexico, Turkey, Czech, Poland, Malaysia, Korea, Hungary, Colombia, Peru, the U.A.E., Chile, Taiwan, South Africa, Brazil, Russia, Thailand, the Philippines, Indonesia, China, and India.[59]

While these countries cannot evolve into developed countries overnight, how far they have come is remarkable. Most of these countries are expected to surpass Canada in size soon. It is important to note that they are not just threatening to surpass Canada in absolute economic size (GDP) but also in terms of incomes per person (GDP per capita). If Canada remains complacent, it could be left even further behind. Technology has largely set the global economic growth standard, and it's just a matter of how a country wants to plug in and play. But the global economic game isn't stopping for anyone.

2001: A Space Odyssey (1967)

Filmed in 1967, 2001 A Space Odyssey showed a future where computers could talk and artificial intelligence was a reality. North America was suburbanizing, and supermarkets were just starting to replace "mom and pop" retailers. The Defense Advanced Research Projects Agency (DARPA) had just started connecting computers, a precursor to the World Wide Web.

That future has now arrived: big box stores (Walmart), artificial intelligence (Google), and ubiquitous computing power. Today, HAL has been replaced by Alexa (Amazon) and Siri (Apple), who manage our access to information, household utilities, and home security.

---

59 Yumi Teso, et al. These are 2018's most (and least) attractive emerging markets. Bloomberg.com, January 21, 2018. https://bloom.bg/2TFdrGY

Amazon with its Whole Foods acquisition and Walmart with its push into the e-commerce space have been entering each other's territories as digital and physical economic worlds continue to converge.

Think ahead to 2067. Stores (if they still exist) will require no check-out. More urban density will be coupled with fewer vehicles as ride-sharing and autonomous vehicles become widespread. Artificial intelligence in quantum computing and ubiquitous broadband access will be common. A rapidly aging, but long-living population will strain our health care system. This will call for increased technology, innovation, and efficiency to improve outcomes and lower health-system costs. We do not know which companies will top the most valued companies list in 2067, but we can make a pretty good guess which industries they will be in.

We need to be investing in the winning trends of the future. Battery technology is a likely candidate. Would Tesla build a new GigaFactory in Canada, given that key components such as cobalt, copper, and lithium are mined here? Not unless we step forward and enable the innovative ecosystem necessary to encourage it. We also need a co-operative government. In July 2022, Tesla filed documents with the Ontario government, stating it was looking to build an "advanced manufacturing facility" in the province.

The World's Shifting Economic Geography

In 1967, the G7 countries represented more than 60 percent of the global economy. Since then, Asian and emerging market wealth has grown and the world's economic mass has shifted from West to East, and the G7's influence on the global order has fallen significantly.

Table 2 Size of Economies and World GDP Shares: A Shift in the Global Economy

	1967		1992		2017		2019	
	Real GDP	% of World	Real GDP	% of World	Real GDP	% of World	Real GDP	% of World
United States	4,898,779	31.0	10,189,422	22.1	19,754,754	16.5	20,860,506	16.6
Japan	1,053,519	6.7	3,898,342	8.5	5,003,368	4.2	5,028,348	4.0
United Kingdom	832,711	5.3	1,402,815	3.0	3,037,791	2.5	3,118,991	2.5
Germany	1,045,258	6.6	2,434,019	5.3	4,237,503	3.5	4,308,862	3.4
France	778,855	4.9	1,617,569	3.5	2,922,007	2.4	3,018,885	2.4
Italy	569,271	3.6	1,641,885	3.6	2,474,221	2.1	2,508,405	2.0
Canada	389,248	2.5	901,134	2.0	1,771,273	1.5	1,846,581	1.5
G7		60.5		48.0		32.8		32.4
Brazil	282,003	1.8	1,069,874	2.3	2,970,571	2.5	3,089,274	2.5
Russian Federation			2,423,958	5.3	3,907,710	3.3	4,197,223	3.3
India	669,394	4.2	1,341,249	2.9	8,069,978	6.8	8,945,547	7.1
China	898,740	5.7	3,311,326	7.2	19,501,140	16.3	20,056,066	16.0
BRIC		NA		17.7		28.8		28.9

Source: Penn World Tables, Expenditure-side real GDP at chained PPPs (in mil. 2017US$).

By 1992, the G7 share had fallen to 48 percent, and in 2017 it was 33 percent. Over the same period, the BRIC economies—Brazil, Russia, India, and China—increased their share of the global economy from approximately 12 percent to almost 30 percent. While the pace of growth of emerging economies will ultimately slow, their growth rates will likely remain relatively elevated for some time. We are in the midst of a continued shift in the world's economic activity and power from West to East and North to South

Canada's Economic Size: Falling in Importance Globally

Former Prime Minister Paul Martin recognized the importance of Canadian membership in the G7 early on, but realized that such an exclusive group wasn't sustainable in a rapidly changing global economy.

Table 3 Canada's Rank on Real GDP, 1967, 2017, and 2067 (billions of US$, PPP)

	1967			*2017*			*2067*	
Rank	*Country*	*Real GDP (PPP)*	*Rank*	*Country*	*Real GDP (PPP)*	*Rank*	*Country*	*Real GDP (PPP)*
1	United States	4,899	1	United States	19,755	1	India	97,402
2	Japan	1,054	2	China	19,501	2	China	94,215
3	Germany	1,045	3	India	8,070	3	United States	45,581
4	China	899	4	Japan	5,003	4	Indonesia	19,195
5	United Kingdom	833	5	Germany	4,238	5	Mexico	11,776

6	France	779	6	Russian Federation	3,908	6	Brazil	11,695
7	India	669	7	United Kingdom	3,038	7	Russia	9,683
8	Italy	569	8	Brazil	2,971	8	Nigeria	8,726
9	Canada	389	9	France	2,922	9	Pakistan	8,645
10	Mexico	382	10	Indonesia	2,819	10	Egypt	8,403
11	Spain	327	11	Italy	2,474	11	Turkey	8,294
12	Brazil	282	12	Mexico	2,405	12	Saudi Arabia	7,699
13	Australia	224	13	Turkey	2,107	13	Japan	7,607
14	Netherlands	210	14	Republic of Korea	2,071	14	Germany	7,523
15	Turkey	208	15	Spain	1,853	15	United Kingdom	7,367
16	Switzerland	166	16	Canada	1,771	16	Vietnam	7,201
17	South Africa	162	17	Saudi Arabia	1,613	17	Philippines	6,626
18	Sweden	147	18	Australia	1,240	18	Bangladesh	6,621
19	Belgium	140	19	Thailand	1,172	19	Iran	6,304
20	Indonesia	104	20	Iran	1,144	20	France	6,110
21	Austria	96	21	Poland	1,142	21	Malaysia	5,002
22	Nigeria	93	22	Taiwan	1,125	22	South Africa	4,808
23	Iran	92	23	Argentina	1,026	23	South Korea	4,713
24	Bangladesh	92	24	Egypt	1,005	24	Thailand	4,242
25	Denmark	90	25	Nigeria	967	25	Canada	4,158

GDP 1967 and 2017, Expenditure-side real GDP at chained PPPs (in mil. 2017 US$) taken from Penn World Table Version 10.0.

GDP 2067: Computed by taking CAGR of GDP projections in 2050 from PwC, *The World in 2050* over GDP 2017 figures from IMF WEO April 2017 data and applying it over 2017 figures until 2067.

As China, India, and other emerging markets represented larger shares of the global economy, it became imperative that a new group emerge, to better reflect and represent these new global realities. As a member of an expanded G20, Canada "was firmly anchored, and Canada's role in helping forge it gave it special prominence."[60] In the future, the question arises whether Canada can maintain sufficient economic prominence and size to continue to be a meaningful member of this group in the coming decades. Table 3 indicates that the answer to this question is no. Canada will soon fall off the list of the world's top 20 largest economies.

Prosperity

In any society, the more prosperous its people, the better quality of life they will have. How we pursue and measure prosperity will be important to shaping the right policies to attain it. There is an active policy debate on the importance of absolute size of an economy (GDP) as an indicator of success or whether the focus instead should be on incomes per person (GDP per capita). Those who focus on GDP per capita argue that the focus should be on making Canada smart, affluent, and optimizing our existing resources and people, as opposed to simply becoming larger by increasing immigration.

Let's explore these two paradigms.

How is Canada doing on incomes per person? As Table 4 indicates, in 1967, Canada's income per person was third in the world, second only to Switzerland and the United States. In 2017, Canada's rank

60 John Ibbitson and Tara Perkins, How Canada made the G20 happen. *The Globe and Mail*, May 1, 2018. https://tgam.ca/33GGi2d

Table 4 Canada's Declining Rank on GDP per Capita, PPP (Excludes Countries with Populations Less Than 5 Million)

	1967			2017			2067	
Rank	*Country*	*Real GDP/ Cap*	*Rank*	*Country*	*Real GDP/ Cap at PPP*	*Rank*	*Country*	*Real GDP/ Cap at PPP*
1	Switzerland	27,896	1	Singapore	85,554	1	Ireland	185,876
2	United States	24,128	2	Switzerland	70,059	2	United Arab Emirates	151,321
3	Canada	19,025	3	United Arab Emirates	68,235	3	Norway	128,303
4	Australia	18,703	4	Norway	61,759	4	Hong Kong	121,350
5	Sweden	18,679	5	United States	60,768	5	Singapore	116,419
6	Netherlands	16,671	6	China, Hong Kong SAR	59,519	6	Kuwait	111,607
7	France	15,365	7	Sweden	54,982	7	Malaysia	108,502
8	United Kingdom	15,167	8	Austria	54,527	8	Taiwan	105,054
9	Belgium	14,673	9	Netherlands	53,976	9	United States	103,008
10	Germany	13,499	10	Denmark	53,752	10	Netherlands	101,365
11	Austria	12,955	11	Germany	51,265	11	San Marino	99,750
12	Italy	10,838	12	Australia	50,452	12	Germany	95,023
13	Japan	10,391	13	Belgium	49,764	13	United Kingdom	92,633
14	Spain	9,966	14	Saudi Arabia	48,744	14	Poland	91,491

15	Greece	8,782	15	Canada	48,221	15	Australia	89,639
16	Mexico	8,148	16	Taiwan	47,766	16	Austria	89,639
17	Venezuela	8,107	17	Finland	46,026	17	Sweden	88,783
18	South Africa	7,964	18	United Kingdom	45,525	18	Switzerland	86,478
19	Chile	7,130	19	France	43,597	19	Denmark	85,304
20	Portugal	6,547	20	Israel	40,977	20	Saudi Arabia	82,630
21	Turkey	6,392	21	Italy	40,779	21	South Korea	79,052
22	Algeria	5,127	22	Republic of Korea	40,530	22	Canada	78,566

GDP per capita 1967: Derived by dividing expenditure-side real GDP at chained PPPs (in mil. 2017 US$) by the country population, both taken from Penn World Table 10.0.

GDP per capita 2067: Obtained by using The Economist Intelligence Unit's long-term outlook on GDP per capita growth on world's highest GDP/capita and fast growth emerging countries.

dropped significantly, down to 15th, whereas the United States fell only to 5th place. This trend is projected to continue over the coming fifty years, where Canada's rank is expected to fall to 22nd whereas the United States is expected to remain in the top ten.

These projections do not fully reflect the rise of the digital economy, the increasing importance of innovation and the diminishing importance of fossil fuels. The projections also don't factor in the rise of protectionism in the United States, Canada's largest trading partner. Once these factors are taken into account, the outlook for Canada's economy is more concerning. The urgency required to address these threats to Canadian prosperity cannot be underestimated.

In 2017, Canadian average income per person was US$48,221, as compared to income per person in the United States of US$60,768.

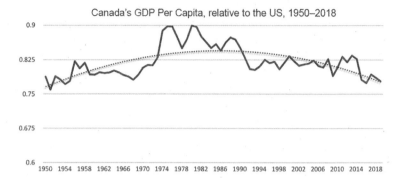

Figure 1 Incomes in Canada relative to those in the United States continue to slide

Source: Data retrieved from the Penn World Tables, version 10.0.

This means that Canada's GDP per person would have to increase by 26 percent to match that in the United States and reflects the *Canadian prosperity discount.* As reflected in Figure 1, the trends indicate that the Canadian prosperity discount is expected to continue to grow unless significant policy changes, such as those advanced in this book, are pursued.

Imagine what it would mean if Canada had the same income per person as the United States, closing the prosperity discount, Canada's overall GDP would be a full 26 percent higher, rising from $1.771 trillion to $2.21 trillion, and increasing Canada's rank globally in 2017 from 16th to 13th place. Further, Canada's rank on income per capita would rise from 15th in the world to 5th, matching that of the United States.

Closing this prosperity gap with the United States would allow Canadians to optimize their potential. It would also mean increased government tax revenue, even at reduced tax rates. By growing incomes per person, governments at the federal and provincial levels would be able to use the increased tax revenue on infrastructure spending. Given that Canadians are less satisfied with access to health care than Americans,[61] more money could be spent to improve the provision of health care services, including addressing the significant wait times for special procedures. More money could also be used for the development of vaccines, and to ensure Canadians have 21st-century skills to plug into the modern economy. And more funds could be allocated to help the Canadian economy shift away from those 20th-century drivers of prosperity to 21st-century drivers of prosperity, including further development of Canada's digital infrastructure, and to generally fund the improvement of Canada's innovation and start-up ecosystems.

All of these policy initiatives could be pursued while reducing the very large personal tax burdens Canadians face. As Table 4 shows, the average incomes in other countries are surpassing those in Canada—other countries are embracing 21st-century drivers of prosperity to a far greater extent than is Canada.

Clearly, change and strategic transformation is needed that will allow Canadians to benefit from the economic and digital revolution.

---

61 See: https://www.cbc.ca/news/health/canada-health-care-access-1.6574184. Only 15 percent of Canadians satisfied with access to care, while 29 percent of Americans satisfied with access.

4

Transition Economy: Resources, Technology, and Talent

You must be the change you wish to see in the world.

—Mahatma Gandhi

In 2012, Murray Edwards, executive chairman of Canadian Natural Resources and co-owner of the Calgary Flames hockey team, asked Annette Verschuren, CEO of NRStor and Canadian Business Hall of Fame inductee, to join the board of Canada's biggest independent oil and gas company.

"Murray," she said, "I'm in the energy storage business. I'm totally the opposite of what you want."

"No, you're not, Annette," he said. "You're the future. And I know that it's going in that direction. How do we make that happen?"

Edwards was right about it being the future. The clean tech industry is growing at a rapid pace. The sector was worth $880 billion in 2008 globally. By 2022 it had grown to more than $2 trillion.[62]

---

62 Canada needs to boost its clean technology sector. *The Globe and Mail*, February 22, 2021.

Meanwhile, the traditional oil and gas business in Canada still employs 800,000 people. How to reconcile industries that appear to be opposites?

As their conversation suggested, there is hope that it is possible to integrate these two disparate elements in the best interests of both old and new. Alberta is a microcosm of many of the issues facing the entire country: the management of legacy resources, technological innovation, diversification, and the need to expand our export markets. These are important transitions that need to be made across the country in many of our traditional industries, whether the energy industry in the West, the auto industry in Ontario, or the fisheries in the East.

Alberta's Energy Economy: A Case Study in the Urgency of Transition

Canada's energy and mining sectors account for 27 percent of the TSX Composite, Canada's flagship index. This compares with 7.6 percent for natural resource companies in the U.S. S&P 500 index. The Canadian resources number is disproportionately high while the technology and health care sectors make up a much smaller proportion of the index, contributing 5.2 percent and 1.7 percent, respectively. Technology companies form nearly 22 percent of the S&P 500, while health care contributes about 14 percent.

The outsized presence of natural resources suggests it is a clear strength, but it also points to the narrow nature of the Canadian market. With technology impacting every industry, it makes sense for Canada to claim its share of the pie. At 5.2 percent of the Canadian market, and about 4.4 percent of the economy, Canada's technology industry has a lot of room to grow. Canada cannot abandon one for the other but needs to combine them; ensure our natural resources sectors are developed with cutting-edge environmental technology, and at the same time aggressively expand our technology presence.

"As the world transitions to a cleaner economy," Prime Minister Justin Trudeau wrote in an email interview, "there will still be demand for our existing resources, and there are hundreds of thousands of good jobs that currently depend on it. We need to get those resources to market, but we also need to chart a path forward to a cleaner economy that is less reliant on fossil fuels."

For the most part, the oil industry agrees. Greg Stringham, vice-president of Markets and Oil Sands for the Canadian Association of Petroleum Producers (CAPP), noted that it is only recently that the industry has steered its considerable resources towards sustainability. "The in-situ oil sands operation only became commercially viable around 1990," he said. "So technology was really focused on extraction until the early to mid-2000s, then we said, you know what, we need to focus on environmental sustainability." Oil is a capital-intensive industry with long timelines, and it can take years for new technologies to work through the system and register gains.

The oil sands had a long period of development, then a glorious, profitable moment in the sun before becoming the poster child for climate change, unfairly shouldering the sins of an entire industry. They are struggling with critical pipeline battles and have lost the narrative and the PR battle. That battle initially pitted them against Amnesty International and celebrity detractors like Leonardo DiCaprio, Jane

Fonda, and Neil Young (who called the oil sands "Hiroshima").[63] Alberta's initial response was to set up a government-funded "War Room" with a budget of $30 million to attack its attackers.[64] Critics were labelled "eco-terrorists" and foreign agitators.

This schoolyard approach didn't do anything to sway public opinion and most importantly, alienated potential oil customers by essentially arguing with them. And now the activists are no longer just Hollywood celebrities and environmental agencies, they are fund managers and corporations. Larry Fink, CEO of BlackRock, which has over US$8 trillion in assets under management, wrote an open letter to CEOs where he noted that "climate risk is investment risk," and that the reallocation of capital was accelerating faster than he had expected.[65] In 2020, investments in sustainable assets were up by 96 percent over the previous year. And these companies are increasingly profitable. "During 2020," Fink wrote, "81% of a globally-representative selection of sustainable indexes outperformed their parent benchmarks." It is, he wrote, a tectonic shift. "I believe that this is the beginning of a long but rapidly accelerating transition—one that will unfold over many years and reshape asset prices of every type . . . we believe the climate transition presents a historic investment opportunity"[66] . . . "Every

---

63 Neil Young calls Fort McMurray oilsands 'a wasteland. *CBC News*, September 10, 2013. https://www.cbc.ca/news/entertainment/neil-young-calls-fort-mcmurray-oilsands-a-wasteland-1.1701227#:~:text=Canadian%20singer%2Dsongwriter%20Neil%20Young

64 Drew Anderson, Alberta's energy "war room" launches in Calgary. CBC News, December 11, 2019. https://www.cbc.ca/news/canada/calgary/alberta-war-room-launch-calgary-1.5392371

65 Larry Fink, Larry Fink's 2020 letter to CEOs: A fundamental reshaping of finance. Blackrock. https://www.blackrock.com/us/individual/larry-fink-ceo-letter

66 Ibid.

company and every industry will be transformed by the transition to a net-zero world. The question is, will you lead, or will you be led?"[67]

Fink's position was lauded by environmental groups, but the bottom line was more complicated. BlackRock retained significant investments in oil and gas, and still had $85 billion invested in coal companies. Oil is a conflicting force; we want to reduce our carbon footprint but still remain energy secure and profit from our natural resources the world will continue to need. We want to reduce emissions and still stay warm in our cold winters or fly to Florida in January. But the long-term investment trend is clear. BlackRock, as well as many other money managers representing tens of trillions of dollars, is committed to the goal of net-zero greenhouse gas emissions by 2050 or sooner.

In 2020, 54 percent of cars sold in Norway were electric vehicles (EVs); only 17 percent were gas or diesel powered, the rest hybrids. In 2021, EVs represented 64.5 percent of all car sales, and in 2022 the figure will top 70 percent. While EVs make up a relatively small part of the vehicle mix globally (less than 3 percent), every major car manufacturer has developed one or more, and Tesla quickly became the largest car company in the world as measured by market capitalization. Also, California recently announced that it wants to ban the sale of gas vehicles by 2035.[68] What if China is the next Norway or California? The Chinese government has built more than 1.42 million electric charging stations in the country, and the rate of

67 Larry Fink, Larry Fink's 2022 letter to CEOs: The power of capitalism. Blackrock. https://www.blackrock.com/corporate/investor-relations/larry-fink-ceo-letter
68 See https://www.npr.org/2022/08/27/1119360031/california-gas-cars-electric-cars-zero-emission-climate-change

construction is accelerating; in May 2022 alone, they built 87,000 new stations. The China Association of Automobile Manufacturers reported that sales of EVs, hybrids, and hydrogen fuel cell vehicles would increase by 40 percent in 2021. In fact, sales of EVs in China increased by 169.1 percent in 2021. The future may arrive sooner than we think.

It isn't just investors and consumers, but corporations that are pivoting towards sustainability. General Motors plans to build only zero-emission cars by 2035 and is putting $27 billion towards the transition as well as helping develop a charging network. Jaguar, Volvo, and almost all other car manufacturers have set ambitious EV goals.

For the Alberta government to lash out at detractors is to attack the market, its customers, and potential investors. It was waging a war against not just the market, but the future. Energy-efficient products will dominate the market, not because of good intentions, but because they are better products. Why would we want to continue to have to stop and fill up our cars at a gas station which are essentially dangerous biohazard sites?

Oil sands producers are looking for clarity from governments rather than protection. When Rachel Notley's government presented a climate change policy, it was embraced by oil sands. They saw it as an opportunity rather than an impediment. At the time, Murray Edwards said, "This plan will position Alberta, one of the world's largest oil and gas producing jurisdictions, as a climate leader and will allow for ongoing innovation and technology in the oil and gas sector."[69]

Right now, the rest of the world isn't much interested in the oil

---

69 C. Turner, *The patch: The people, pipelines, and politics of the oil sands.* Simon and Schuster, 2017. p. 289.

sands. The withdrawal began in 2016, with Statoil pulling out. Royal Dutch Shell sold most of its oil sands assets in 2017 and announced it would invest $1 billion annually in renewable energy. Exxon, Imperial, ConocoPhillips, and Marathon all cut back or pulled out. Even the Koch Brothers, notorious climate-change deniers, scrapped plans for an oil sands project near Fort McMurray.[70]

Despite this exodus, the oil sands remain a valuable economic resource, and Alberta could have a productive second act.

There is general agreement that it will be decades before the world weans itself off oil and the war in Ukraine has highlighted the complexities in transition and energy security where desperation has driven people back to burning coal. The oil sands are one of the largest deposits in the world, and Canada is arguably the most stable and democratic oil-producing country. The hard reality is today the United States no longer needs Canada's oil because of the fracking revolution. And that forms the background against which any pipeline approval decisions are being made in the United States, including the Keystone Pipeline project. Whenever a customer doesn't need something, the decision to close your store becomes a lot easier. However, that revolution may not be sustainable because fracking is also environmentally intrusive (banned in several European countries), and fracked wells tend to have a short production life.[71] More critically, fracking is unprofitable at lower oil prices.

---

70 Patrick DeRochie, Seven oil multinationals that are pulling out of Canada's tar sands. Environmental Defence. March 14, 2017. https://environmentaldefence. ca/2017/03/14/seven-oil-multinationals-pulling-canadas-tar-sands/

71 Michael Lynch, How is U.S. shale oil production performing so well? *Forbes*, June 21, 2021. https://www.forbes.com/sites/michaellynch/2021/06/21/ how-is-us-shale-oil-production-performing-so-well/?sh=62af23c36e08

In 2019, the *Wall Street Journal* reported that the break-even price for fracking was $49 per barrel, and it estimated that the industry had already lost $300 billion. A 2020 report from the accounting firm Deloitte predicted that it would lose another $300 billion. In 2020, Chesapeake Energy, a fracking pioneer, and one of the largest oil and gas companies, declared bankruptcy.

The war in Ukraine has renewed U.S. interest in foreign oil supplies, and getting it delivered by a friendly neighbour via pipeline is politically more palatable than importing from Saudi Arabia or Venezuela, and environmentally more sustainable than loading it into tankers. This leaves opportunity for Alberta and Canada if we can change the narrative and turn the corner to become leaders in both environmentally responsible extraction and renewable energy solutions.

Canada has committed to a 40 percent reduction in emissions from 2005 levels by 2020, and an 80 percent reduction by 2050. Since the Paris Accord in 2016, five of the G7 countries have reduced emissions. Only Canada and the United States have increased them, with Canada the worst offender (a 3.3 percent increase). The Canada Energy Regulator (CER) calculated that if every Canadian industry other than oil went to net zero, the emissions from oil and gas alone would still cause us to miss the 2050 target by 32 percent. To try and meet our targets and to ensure the economic viability of the oil sands, we need to innovate now more than ever.

Innovation

Innovation is key, and to facilitate it, the Canadian Oil Sands Innovation Alliance (COSIA) was formed in 2012.[72] They looked at incremental technologies (improvements in steam efficiency, reducing water use, reducing emissions) as well as transformative technologies that could radically change how hydrocarbons are turned into energy. While tens of millions have gone into research, it still isn't enough. To frame it in a colloquial way, Canada spends more on Christmas than it does on energy R&D.

According to the report *Towards a More Innovative Future: Insights from Canada's Natural Resources Sector*, "There's more potential for innovation in the natural resources sector than in any other industry, and ultimately, a lot more on the line for society. 'There is an imperative to innovate in this sector because the stakes are higher— not just for sustainable economic growth, but for solutions to the very real challenges facing humanity and the planet.'"[73]

Low-cost, reliable energy is the life blood of any economy and is needed to fuel growth. Oil, gas, hydro, wind, and other energy sources are literally the fuel powering the economy. These sources must proliferate across the economy and must be made available at globally competitive prices for anyone to be economically productive. We possess arguably the greatest abundance of natural resources on

---

72 Canada's Oil Sands Innovation Alliance, Canada's oil sands producers launch environmental performance alliance. March 1, 2012. https://cosia.ca/resources/news-releases/canadas-oil-sands-producers-launch-environmental-performance-alliance

73 Barrie Mckenna, Hewers of wood, maybe; but good at it: report. *The Globe and Mail*, April 2, 2012. https://www.theglobeandmail.com/report-on-business/economy/economy-lab/hewers-of-wood-maybe-but-good-at-it-report/article610507/

the plant. What we don't always have is the greatest management of these resources. Shockingly, Canadian businesses don't have great access to cheap and reliable electricity. According to the World Bank's *Doing Business*, in 2020, Canada ranked 124th in the world in terms of getting access to electricity.[74] How can this be, given our natural energy sources? But the World Bank uses other criteria—the cost of electricity, the length of time it takes to get hooked up, and other metrics as well. There are several reasons for our poor ranking, but government gridlock and mismanagement play a key role.

Perrin Beatty, president and CEO of the Canadian Chamber of Commerce, stated that the demand for oil will fall as electric cars become more prevalent, but the demand for other resources that go into making EVs will rise. "Electric vehicles need three times as much copper wiring as gas powered models," Beatty said. "Elon Musk expects his company will need to absorb the world's entire supply of lithium to meet his annual production goal for Tesla 3s."[75] This is encouraging given the wide diversity and depth of Canada's natural resources. Canada must be equipped not simply to export natural resources to foreign markets where the high-end processing will take place. Canada must deploy policies that encourage the production of more processed natural resources and related higher value innovative activities within Canada. As John Ruffolo, Founder & Managing Partner, Maverix Private Equity eloquently stated, "I kept on saying guys looking at our industrial history, it's funny we have gone back to our roots of a

---

74 World Bank, Doing Business Database. 2020. https://archive.doingbusiness.org/en/data/exploreeconomies/canada

75 Perrin Beatty Speaking Notes, *The Future of Canadian Natural Resources,* Premier's BC Natural Resource Forum, February 2, 2017, Prince George, British Columbia.

hundred and fifty years ago. There's a little but still taking something here, pulling it out of the ground in a non-sustainable way and then not even processing or refining the damn thing here but sending it out and then buying back the finished goods at three to ten x the value. That I can tell you is not the path to prosperity,"

Below is a list of Canadian minerals ordered in terms of value of exports for 2018 (gold, iron and steel, aluminium, copper, miscellaneous metal products, coal and coke, potash and potassium compounds, nickel, iron ore, diamonds, uranium and thorium, zinc, silver, platinum group metals, and all other minerals). Natural Resources Canada categorizes Canada's mineral trade for each of the following four manufacturing stages:

- Stage 1: Mineral extraction products
- Stage 2: Smelting and refining products
- Stage 3: Semi-fabricated products
- Stage 4: Fabricated products

As demonstrated in Table 5, Canada's trade balance is generally large and positive for Stages 1 and 2, but negative for Stages 3 and 4.[76] In other words, Canada's exports in natural resources are disproportionately focused on less processed (raw exports), and its imports are disproportionately focused on processed natural resources. An important additional area for value creation within Canada would involve undertaking more high-end processing of Canadian mineral extracts within Canada.

76 Natural Resources Canada, Mineral trade. https://www.nrcan.gc.ca/maps-tools-and-publications/publications/minerals-mining-publications/mineral-trade/19310#trade

Table 5 Mineral and Metal Trade by Stage ($ billions), 2020

Stage	Domestic Exports	Total Exports	Total Imports	Balance of Trade
Stage 1: Primary products	32.2	32.2	10.1	22.1
Stage 2: Smelting and refining products	38.9	39.1	19.7	19.4
Stage 3: Semi-fabricated products	14.9	16.6	23.2	-6.6
Stage 4: Fabricated products	16.1	18.3	38.0	-19.7
Total Minerals and Metals	102.0	106.3	91.1	15.2

Source: Mineral Trade, Natural Resources Canada, Government of Canada. https://www.nrcan.gc.ca/maps-tools-and-publications/publications/minerals-mining-publications/mineral-trade/19310#trade

Innovation needs to be a concerted effort among industry, government, and academia. Stephen Larter, the Canada Research Chair in Petroleum Geology at the University of Calgary, said that a massive joint effort is needed. "You can't solve the problem using the current business model," he said. "We need a Manhattan Project commitment of resources." The race to build the atomic bomb involved tens of thousands of people, $2 billion (roughly $25 billion in today's dollars) and was conceived, built, and tested within three years. "The Manhattan Project came out of crisis. We need crises to change."

We have crises in the form of wildfires, floods, disappearing glaciers, and devastating heat waves, but for many people, it is still happening offstage. The other thing we need, Larter said, is long-term government policies.

Energy policies have a tortured and divisive history in this country. Decades after it was scrapped, Pierre Trudeau's National Energy Program is still reviled in Alberta. Justin Trudeau's carbon tax found similar resistance. But in the wake of the Supreme Court ruling that the federal government can legislate to prevent existential environmental threats, a new consensus and concerted effort from industry and government is necessary. New technology and legacy resources need to act together for the benefit of everyone. The "resources vs. technology" argument needs to merge into one.

In their report *Technological Prospects for Reducing the Environmental Footprint of the Canadian Oil Sands*, the Council of Canadian Academies noted, "Improvements in environmental performance are likely to be incremental rather than transformative in the near to midterm. The deployment of new technologies being piloted could reduce energy use significantly, and with that GHG emissions by 15 to 35 percent."[77] Nevertheless, there are those who continue to work on transformative technologies.

At the University of Calgary, Dr. Steven Bryant, the Canada Excellence Research Chair in Materials Engineering for Unconventional Oil Reservoirs, was working on nanotechnology to make the oil sands more environmentally efficient. "Longer term," he said, "we're looking at completely different technologies to derive value from the oil sands. We have built a civilization that hinges on one energy transformation— you take a hydrocarbon and set fire to it. What if we still wanted to get energy out of the oil sands, but the energy carrier wasn't a hydrocarbon molecule? What if we could do a transformation in situ; take the chemical energy that's there and convert it to an electron? Microbes do this all the time. What if we could convert that chemical energy into

---

77 Council of Canadian Academies, Technological prospects for reducing the environmental footprint of Canadian Oil Sands, 2015. p. 171–2. https://cca-reports.ca/wp-content/uploads/2018/10/oilsandsfullreporten.pdf

a different form of chemical energy—methane molecules, hydrogen molecules—and still get energy out. Then you'd leave the carbon in place. How sweet is that?"

It is very sweet indeed, though like most transformative technologies, it is difficult to attach a timeline, and time is of the essence. "Right now," he said, "Alberta is this crucible for all the problems facing society in the next century. And some of those problems are in conflict with one another."

To address these conflicts, the University of Calgary has 280 faculty members involved in energy-related research. And there is a concerted effort to turn that research into commercially viable applications. "The whole thing I've done with the research programme is try and push things out the door," said Bryant, "You can move at the speed of business instead of at the speed of graduate students with their dissertations."

There are interesting developments coming out of Alberta's universities, but they aren't getting much traction in the oil industry. "One of the things about the oil sands right now," Bryant said, "is the zeitgeist has shifted and folks are not looking at building a new anything." Any new technology has to fit in with whatever exists.

But incremental gains won't be enough to solve the emissions problem. Dr. Ian Gates is a professor in the Department of Chemical and Petroleum Engineering and director of the University of Calgary's $75 million Global Research Initiative in Sustainable Low Carbon Unconventional Resources. "I always tell the folks downtown [oil executives] that the last 50 years of wealth-creation with respect to oil and gas are not going to be the next 50 years of wealth-creation," he said. "We have to shift to be cleaner. Globally, the world is moving on. There are massive forces which are leading to a sense of low-carbon resources. We've seen lower emissions, but we need to accelerate it."

The industry is looking to carbon capture (CCUS) to solve most of its emissions issues, a good news/bad news technology. The good news is it reduces emissions (CO_2, nitrogen oxide, sulphur dioxide). The bad news is that it's energy intensive (the processes of separation, transportation, and injection into the earth), and if the captured CO_2 is used for enhanced oil recovery—getting more oil out of existing wells—then it may actually add to emissions (though it would reduce the number of new wells being drilled). The view in the scientific community is that there is a place for CCUS, but it is only part of the solution.

When oil was at $40 a barrel, there was little appetite or available capital for innovation. But after the Russian invasion of Ukraine, oil spiked to more than $100 and brought new profits to the oil sands producers. "If the oil companies are serious about decarbonizing," said Stephen Larter, "we'll see that revenue stream going into mitigating existing emissions, new clean technology and an urgent energy transition away from where they are today. If they're not serious about it, then we'll see stock buybacks and executive bonuses and all the usual stuff. It's a good time to watch what they do, not what they say."

Meanwhile, the renewable sector in Alberta is growing exponentially: in 2018, renewables made up only 6 percent of the province's energy mix. In 2022, it had grown to 26 percent and will bring an estimated $3.75 billion worth of investment, along with 4,500 jobs. Within the energy industry, there is a growing diversification, but this needs to increase in order to compete globally.[78]

---

78 (https://www.stalberttoday.ca/local-news/renewable-power-market-booming-in-alberta-experts-5512327).

Diversification

In the 1970s, Alberta Premier Peter Lougheed promised to diversify Alberta's economy. That didn't really happen, and subsequent efforts by other administrations fell short. When the price of oil was high, there was little impetus to diversify; when it collapsed, there was little money to do so. Alberta's strategy for diversification could be reduced to a popular bumper sticker from the 1980s: "Please God, give us another oil boom and we promise not to piss it away this time."[79]

"Whether it's by design or by accident, every natural resource producer in the world wants to diversify," said Scotiabank Chief Economist Jean-François Perrault. "Even Saudi Arabia wants to diversify."

Saudi Arabia has plans to construct some of the largest solar fields in the world, and is building a net-zero emissions city, NEOM. The United Arab Emirates is building Masdar City, a net-zero carbon city. On the corporate front, BP, one of the world's largest oil companies, is pivoting into clean energy, with the goal of being carbon neutral by 2050, and now sports a green flower as its logo. In 2020, the European Union used more renewable energy than fossil fuels for the first time.[80]

Solar energy is cheaper than gas in some markets, and clean energy technologies have adoption rates that are far quicker than the cumbersome oil sands, which can take eight to ten years from research to implementation (though researchers are working to bring that down to under five years). There is an urgency to address these challenges.

---

79 Martin Pelletier, Oil investors must not be complacent — we are not out of the woods yet. *Financial Post,* October 11, 2016.
80 European Commission, State of the Energy Union 2021: Renewables overtake fossil fuels as the EU's main power source. October 26, 2021. https://ec.europa.eu/commission/presscorner/detail/en/ip_21_5554

Diversification is not an easy job, but Alberta is in a strong position to become a clean energy force. Calgary has the highest number of sunshine hours of any Canadian city (2,396 per year), and anyone who has experienced a chinook or visited Lethbridge knows how much wind there is. Alberta could be a leader in wind and solar energy. It also has a young, educated, entrepreneurial population that is equipped to implement green strategies.

The creation of the oil sands was a remarkable feat of innovation, engineering, and financial faith. To have a viable future, Alberta needs to employ some of that same "get'er done" spirit and energy.

The oil sands began in the 1960s as a heavily subsidized Canadian venture that many thought was a fool's errand. It may end that way if not managed properly. Of the foreign companies that pulled out of the oil sands ($30 billion exiting between 2016 and 2019), some did so just to be rid of the growing stigma of "dirty oil." Government has a key role to play, but lashing out at every critic and setting up straw men isn't a path to prosperity. A combination of technology and leadership is needed to secure its future. Without innovation and a new future-focused narrative, there will be less access to foreign investment and capital markets.

"Too often people talk about two separate solitudes—like there's the new economy and there's the old economy," said Victor Dodig, CEO of CIBC, one of Canada's largest banks. "Too often people want to turn away from the old economy, yet it's paying most of the tax bills today. We talk about gas. We talk about oil, hydro-power, all in separate dossiers. We never think about it as one dossier. How can we build a portfolio of energy across the country?"

Dominic Barton, former global managing partner of McKinsey, said that there's a lot of technology to be applied to natural resources. "It's one of the biggest areas of actual innovation because of technology," he said. "[We] are going to have to figure it out, but if we can't get the innovated product out, it doesn't mean anything."

Expanding Markets

Alberta's landlocked oil is a vivid illustration of the downside of our dependence on trade with the United States. We essentially have one customer. As the *Globe and Mail* pointed out, it was essentially a bet on the outcome of the U.S. presidential election,[81] the equivalent of going into a casino and putting it all on black at the roulette wheel. Except it came up red. During his campaign, Joe Biden had promised to kill the Keystone project on his first day in office. Every politician knew that reneging on this promise during the first few hours of his presidency was politically untenable for Biden, especially when he felt he didn't need what we're selling. Yet when the inevitable happened, then Premier Jason Kenney lashed out at Biden and others, including Michigan Governor Gretchen Whitmer, who he suggested was "brain dead"[82] (and who was co-chair of Biden's presidential campaign). He called for retaliation and blamed Ottawa for inaction.

But even if Trump had been re-elected, primarily betting on another pipeline to the United States was short-sighted. The long-term need is for a wider market. For that, the pipeline needs to go to the coast and provide access to Asian and European markets. This need became

---

81 Gary Mason, Jason Kenney's bet on Keystone was a taxpayer-funded trip to the casino. *The Globe and Mail*, Opinion, January 26, 2021.

82 Graham Thomson, OPINION | Kenney faces headache and humiliation as Biden prepares to kill Keystone XL, CBC News, January 19, 2021. https://www.cbc.ca/news/canada/edmonton/opinion-kenney-faces-headache-and-humiliation-as-biden-prepares-to-kill-keystone-xl-1.5878472

agonizingly clear after Vladimir Putin's invasion of Ukraine and his subsequent weaponizing of energy. When the European Union joined the United States in imposing sanctions, Putin responded with the threat of cutting off energy supplies to Europe, which gets more than a third of its gas from Russia. Germany, the largest European economy, is most affected: more than half its gas, 53 percent of its oil, and 34 percent of its coal comes from Russia. This dependence on an authoritarian regime has proven to be one of the European Union's greatest miscalculations. It made clear how quickly the global energy market can be manipulated, with billions of people facing shortages and/or price hikes of several hundred percent. It also made it clear how important energy independence is.

Energy independence isn't possible in the near term for most nations, but they could look to Canada as the most stable and reliable source for fossil fuels. However, for that to happen, we need pipelines to the coast. The decision by the federal government to buy the Trans-Mountain pipeline for $4.5 billion was controversial, but it had the advantage, at least, of potentially solving a major problem for Alberta oil: finding diverse markets.

The reality is that the natural resource sectors still make up a significant part of the Canadian economy. Resources account for 11 percent of the country's GDP, half of its exports, 37 percent of foreign investment, and a quarter of capital investment. With a more innovative mindset, we can position ourselves as an energy leader of today and tomorrow. However, we need to build a bridge to that future. What about building our own net-zero emission communities in Canada, starting in Alberta?

Toronto became enamoured with a community development project by Google affiliate Sidewalk Labs that was centred around the idea of data and technology that would be built "from the internet up." The project was later abandoned due to concerns about the data privacy of citizens, among other issues. If we can be seduced by the idea of "internet" cities why not become enamoured with developing net-zero emissions communities in Edmonton and Calgary, in the same way that Saudi Arabia and the UAE have. It would advance our direct national interests in core existing priorities: (i) addressing the existential threats of climate change, (ii) developing needed affordable housing inventory, (iii) resetting our image as "dirty" oil producers, and (iv) helping position and transition Albertans for the energy industry as that bridge to the future as renewable innovation hubs. The initiatives could be undertaken in partnership with both the University of Alberta and University of Calgary harnessing the institutional research power and educating and nurturing the next generation of energy leaders. These projects could also become great potential customers from home-grown renewable energy providers and start-ups to both sponsor their expansion and entry into the global energy industry.

If the transition is managed effectively, Canada could well become one of the few countries poised to responsibly benefit from the global shift from fossil fuels to a technology-driven economy where the most valuable resource is human capital rather than oil. Canada has core strengths in both areas and can use the old economy to fund the new economy. It will create cross-generational benefits, grow our national economy, and provide a framework for shared prosperity from West to East.

The story of the Alberta oil industry is just one example of the transition from past to the future across Canada. The auto industry in Ontario and fisheries in the East are similar examples of what's needed to build a bridge from the past to the future, starting from our historic strong points.

5

The Global Marketplace

There are legitimate concerns and anxieties that the forces of globalisation are leaving too many people behind—and we have to take those concerns seriously and address them. But the answer isn't to turn inward and embrace protectionism. We can't just walk away from trade.

—Barack Obama

As president, Barack Obama rejected protectionism, but his successor embraced it, or at least the idea of it. It is a familiar cry of populist politicians to bring back manufacturing jobs to their own country. While currently being recalibrated, globalization, as both a future social and economic reality, isn't going away. Beyond the populist rhetoric, history has shown that humanity becoming more connected over time is not some short-term trend, but an enduring dynamic of humanity continually facilitated by forces like technology and travel. AP Moller-Maersk is the second largest container shipping company in the world, responsible for one of every six containers on the oceans. Soren Skou, the company's chief executive told the *Financial Times* that Europeans and Americans were actually looking for more Asian suppliers. Trade will shift over the years, but it isn't going away. Trading partners may fall out of favour as politics dictates (China/United States; Russia/almost everyone) but we will continue to trade. And now is a good time to reassess our own trading partners.

"We have for our entire history been attached to the hip to one of the greatest nations and one of the greatest economies history has ever seen," said Grant Kernaghan, Chairman and CEO of Citigroup Global Markets Canada. "That has generally worked very well for Canada."

But Kernaghan warned there is a changing of the guard in terms of the global importance of the United States. "Are we structurally capable of adjusting to those geopolitical changes? Will our geographic location, which has been such a boon to this country over the past 155 years, be a hindrance to us for the next 155 years because we find ourselves too geographically isolated, too culturally isolated?"

Canada's two important natural drivers of prosperity—geography and natural resources—have been a huge advantage until now, but we are approaching a point where these advantages are wearing thin. The U.S. government's aggressive stance in the USMCA negotiations suggests that Canada cannot assume it will always enjoy a priority U.S. relationship. It was a rude wake-up call, though ultimately a necessary one.

Clearly, Canada needs to diversify its economy, both geographically and industry-wise. The C.D. Howe Institute's William B.P. Robson recommended a broad-based approach.

"Trade diversification as a policy suffers from the same fundamental problem as industrial policy," he said. "We don't know over time which parts of the world are going to be the most dynamic, just as we don't know over time which sectors of the economy are going to be the most dynamic. The U.S. may not be the most dynamic market for us in the years ahead, but there's no case for deliberately disengaging with it," he said. "We should be thinking about expanding everywhere."

This means new trade relationships and expanding into growth markets like Asia.

Dominic Barton agreed that Canada needs to engage with the broader world. "We have to double down on the outward focus," he said. "We've got to shift a much more significant proportion of our trade and activity to the Asia region."

This doesn't mean reducing Canada's business with the United States or sacrificing our close relationship, but boosting the percentage of business from other countries. Doug Porter, chief economist at BMO Capital Markets, said Canada shouldn't cut its U.S. business but needs to rather work on strengthening trading relationships with other countries. "(It's) just the law of gravity, the fact that they are right next door, that we are complementary economies. I think it's a dependence that will never go away."

There are Canadian companies that can be considered global leaders. The top Canadian companies by revenue in 2020 are listed in Table 6.

Table 6 Presence of Canadian Companies on the World's 500 Largest Public Companies, 2020

Rank on Fortune 500	Company	Revenues ($M)
155	Brookfield Asset Management	$67,826
181	Manulife Financial	$59,969
183	Alimentation Couche-Tard	$59,118
223	Royal Bank of Canada	$50,863
267	Toronto-Dominion Bank	$44,502
315	Magna International	$39,431
330	George Weston	$37,765
331	Enbridge	$37,735

Rank on Fortune 500	Company	Revenues ($M)
346	Power Corp. of Canada	$36,810
358	Bank of Nova Scotia	$35,101
418	Sun Life Financial	$29,905
427	Suncor Energy	$29,385
430	Bank of Montreal	$29,610

http://fortune.com/global500/list/filtered?hqcountry=Canada

Among these names, a few have managed to build businesses outside of Canada. Companies such as Magna, Couche-Tard, and CGI Group generate more revenue outside Canada than in the country. Toronto-Dominion Bank is a great example of a successful expansion into the U.S. Northeast, managing to create signifiicant brand recognition.

But in an increasingly digital and information-based economy, innovation and creativity are the drivers that create value. Canada has not yet achieved its potential, and in fact is falling further behind.

A More Innovative Canadian Economy
Will Prepare Us for Global Success

The challenge facing the Canadian economy is not just attracting more foreign capital but increasing Canada's reach into the global economy. It's incumbent upon the Canadian government to focus its efforts on emerging markets, including Asia and Africa more broadly. At the same time, policies must be created to help Canadian firms access those markets. This involves improving the innovative capacity and productivity of Canadian companies.

The forces of engagement and competition within Canada, including with foreign companies, will spur innovation. Whether a nation or a business, the more sheltered it is, the less innovative it will be. Based on discussions with stakeholders across the country, we have identified the following bottlenecks to the introduction of more competitive forces within Canada and resulting increased innovation for the Canadian economy.

Haphazard Policies

There is an old joke: How do you start a small business in Canada? The punch line: Start a large business and wait.

Government regulations aren't conducive to small business. There are 1.2 million small- and medium-sized businesses in Canada, and they employ nearly 70 percent of the Canadian labour force. They are critical to innovation in Canada and with the "great resignation" occurring post-COVID-19 it will only grow. Although accompanied by much less fanfare and eye-catching headlines than major plant openings, small businesses have always been the lifeblood of our economy, and in this digital and post-COVID-19 era, this is one area for us to double down on and boost opportunities at home and abroad.

Canadians need access to the resources necessary to succeed without experiencing unnecessary government bureaucracy. There are several government policies that impede the ability of small firms to grow, inhibiting both productivity and innovation. The Canadian Chamber of Commerce's produced a study—Canada's *Top 10 Barriers to Competitiveness in 2016*[83] that cited policies which inhibit the

---

83 Canadian Chamber of Commerce, *Canada's Top 10 Barriers to Competitiveness in 2016.* https://gncc.ca/canadas-top-10-barriers-to-competitiveness-in-2016/

growth of small companies. These include a tax system that punishes small firms once their incomes rise above $500,000. At that point they are no longer eligible for the small business tax of 11 percent and move to the higher 15 percent corporate tax. There are also significant costs associated with complying with highly complex Canadian tax laws, challenges with the administration of the SR&ED technology tax incentive programme and limited small business deductions.

Subject to national security concerns, Canada needs to continue to open more markets through additional trade agreements and liberalize both trade and investment flows, including exports and imports, and outward and inward foreign investment. These agreements reduce the costs and frictions associated with international trade, as well as the risks associated with creating global relationships. This would go a long way towards enhancing the value proposition for Canadian firms to begin trading with these new global markets. But, as Stephen Harper said during the formal announcement of the free trade agreement signed with the EU (the Comprehensive Economic Trade Agreement, CETA), now that the government has opened that market for Canadian business, it is up to business to take advantage of the significant opportunities within Europe.[84] Canadian firms must be prepared to exploit these international opportunities, and be better prepared to compete with imports and foreign businesses operating in Canada.

The second key challenge is developing policies that will enhance productivity and innovation. In a series of studies undertaken by the Government of Canada and the Rotman School of Management, using

---

84 One of the authors of this book attended that meeting, and this comment is extracted from his notes.

data from all firms operating in Canada, the evidence demonstrates that companies participating in the global economy, either by trading or through foreign investment, are far more productive than the firms that are not. These productivity premiums are huge. As shown in Figure 2, firms engaged in the global economy are larger, are more innovative, pay higher wages, and are more capital intensive. As Canadian firms access global markets and grow, they will account for a larger share of the Canadian economy, enhance Canadian economic productivity, and, ultimately, its prosperity.[85]

But in order to participate in the global economy beyond the United States, businesses must start with high productivity. Firms that are exporting or undertaking foreign investment have higher

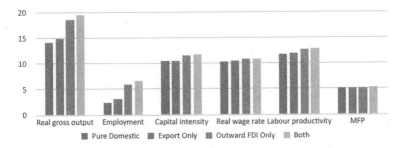

Figure 2 Firms engaged in the global economy are larger, more capital intensive, are more productive, and pay higher wages.

Sources: Outward FDI, Exports, and Firm Performance: Evidence from Canadian Manufacturing. Walid Hejazi (Rotman School of Management, University of Toronto) and Jianmin Tang (Strategy, Research and Results Branch, Innovation, Science, and Economic Development Canada), January 2018, Working Paper.

Note: MFP denotes multifactor productivity, which is a broader measure of productivity than labour productivity.

85 Walid Hejazi, Jianmin Tang, and Weimin Wang, 2021. Selection, learning, and productivity at the firm level: Evidence from Canadian outward FDI. *Journal of International Business Studies*, 52 (2), pp. 306–320.

productivity, not *because* they are engaged in the global economy, but *because* they were productive to begin with due to the disciplining pressures and benefits of global competition. Signing trade deals and gaining access for Canadian firms have more impact and benefit to the economy if Canadian firms are more innovative beforehand—to best take advantage of new market opportunities. As such, we need policies to enable Canadian firms to be more innovative, efficient, and productive. Such policies would go a long way to solving Canada's productivity challenges along with our over-reliance on the U.S. market. Canada would be more innovative in an increasingly digital economy and focus on higher-value processing activities.

Among Organization for Economic Co-operation and Development (OECD) countries, Canada ranks 25th out of 36 on productivity, and continues to lose ground among its peers. The *Globe and Mail* compared Canada's government policies with Australia's.[86] "Australia's systematic productivity framework and institutions contrast with Canada's haphazard and erratic approach." In 1998, Australia created a national Productivity Commission that covers all parts of the economy as well as environmental and social concerns. The Commission's mandate is to "Improve the productivity and economic performance of the economy; reduce unnecessary regulation; encourage the development of efficient and internationally competitive Australian industries; facilitate adjustment to structural change; recognize the interests of the community generally and all those likely to be affected

---

86 David Williams and Jock Finlayson, What Canada can learn from Australia to boost our dismal productivity growth. *The Globe and Mail*, OPINION, January 31, 2021. https://www.theglobeandmail.com/business/commentary/article-what-canada-can-learn-from-australia-to-boost-our-dismal-productivity/

by its proposals; promote regional employment and development; have regard to Australia's international commitments and the trade policies of other countries; and ensure Australian industry develops in ecologically sustainable ways."

This is a wide-ranging mandate, but it has proven effective; Australia's productivity growth is higher than Canada's. And they have a smaller proportion of tech companies. We could take a page from their playbook.

Access to Capital

There are a great many ideas and innovations that weren't commercialized in Canada because of a lack of access to capital, which remains a major barrier for Canadian entrepreneurs.[87] They either don't make it beyond the idea stage, or if they do, they go to the United States, where there are much deeper pools of capital. A great example is Thalmic Labs, one of Canada's most successful start-ups. It raised $158 million, though most of the funds came from the United States. When the company went out for its next round of financing, Canadian VCs were approached, but passed.[88]

Canadian technology companies have managed to become global phenomena, though it appears to be in spite of the system rather than because of it.

---

87 Ipsos Report, Almost three-in-ten citizens globally say they have started a business at some point. July 22, 2022.

88 Catherine McIntyre, Thalmic Labs' $120 million funding round shows the limits of Canada's VCs. *Canadian Business*, October 4, 2016. https://archive. canadianbusiness.com/innovation/thalmic-labs-intel-amazon-funding/

Wattpad, a global platform for writers that has morphed into an entertainment company, surpassed 80 million monthly users in 2019. It raised money in several funding rounds, mostly from U.S. investors. Founder Allen Lau said that as he raised funds, he was asked when, not if, his company would be moving to Silicon Valley. Lau acknowledged the importance of building valuable relationships in the Valley, but managed to stay private without being acquired by a U.S. giant. Lau said it's very hard for a small company to attract the best talent in Silicon Valley. The best talent would go to Facebook and Google. "Why would I want to pay more to get less, right? It just doesn't make sense," said Lau, who believes Wattpad can be "the magnet of attracting the best talent" by being based in Toronto. Wattpad expanded with offices in New York and Los Angeles. In the end, Lau got the best of both worlds, selling the company to South Korean firm Naver for $600 million, with the stipulation that it remains headquartered in Toronto.[89]

It's worth looking at capital through the lens of investment banks. An investment banker interviewed for this book noted, "For many years, I had the privilege to work at a Canadian bank, and hence had the opportunity to see many small companies that had great potential. But the bank's view was they were too small and too early, and hence we lost touch with these companies. But there are many examples of Canadian companies whose success came in the US." He then listed a dozen companies. In recent $100 million type deals, typically $10 million would come from Canada, and the rest from the United States, and the Canadian money would only follow investments from the United States. A large number of successful Canadian companies were funded

89 https://www.theglobeandmail.com/business/article-wattpad-sold-to-south-korean-giant-naver-in-us600-million-plus-deal/

by non-Canadian capital, often with Canadians contributing only after the company had overcome much of the uncertainty of being a start-up. This hesitation on the part of Canadian lenders has led to the arrival in Canada of Silicon Valley Bank, which is expected to fund 40 percent of Canada's tech and life sciences ventures.[90]

The Competition Bureau noted, "the dearth of investment focused on fintech companies is contributing to the exodus of financial services sector innovators seeking more fintech-friendly jurisdictions and putting Canada's global competitiveness at risk." The Big Six banks control roughly 90 percent of the market. "And because of that," said Sue Britton, chief executive and founder of the FinTech Growth Syndicate, "they control (and are slowing) the pace of innovation to a great extent in Canada." There is a lot of talk about innovation but now it's time to act.[91] Jim Balsillie wrote, "Empty talk on innovation is killing Canada's economic prosperity."[92]

90 Stefanie Marotta, Silicon Valley Bank expanding into Quebec with third Canadian office. *Financial Post*, October 12, 2021. https://financialpost.com/fp-finance/banking/silicon-valley-bank-expanding-into-quebec-with-third-canadian-office

91 Geoff Zochodne, How Canada's banking protections stifle innovation at home, but give Big Six free rein to expand abroad. *Financial Post*. July 23, 2018. https://financialpost.com/news/fp-street/how-canadas-banking-protections-stifle-innovation-at-home-but-give-big-six-free-rein-to-expand-abroad

92 Jim Balsillie, Empty talk on innovation is killing Canada's economic prosperity. *The Globe and Mail*, March 17, 2017. https://financialpost.com/news/fp-street/how-canadas-banking-protections-stifle-innovation-at-home-but-give-big-six-free-rein-to-expand-abroad

Unused Government R&D Credits

The Canadian government has tried to help by subsidizing R&D, introducing programmes such as Scientific Research & Experimental Development (SR&ED), yet relatively few companies take advantage of these subsidies. One reason is that the programme is difficult to administer, reflected in the proliferation of companies that provide consulting services to small firms to apply for these benefits. The programme is administered by the Canada Revenue Agency (CRA), which means dealing with tax auditors, which is a disincentive. Applying for the SR&ED credits is equated with a high probability of being audited, with the initial award often being reduced after the fact. There has been no change in the legislation, but the amount of paperwork required is increasing and the eligible expenses are decreasing. Compliance costs are quite high, with as much as 15 percent of tax credits allocated of less than $100,000 going to compliance. CRA is also launching an increasing number of challenges, costing claimants time and resources, thus distracting them from focusing on their innovative businesses.[93]

"The number of Notice of Objection filings taxpayers made to CRA in connection with the Subsidy's related tax credits has 'skyrocketed' over the last several years," read one report. "The data is indicative of a growing disconnect between innovators and the CRA with respect to what sort of activity will attract the Subsidy's tax credits. The

---

93 David Hearn, Statistics Reveal Dramatic Increase in SR&ED Appeals. April 11, 2014. Retrieved from Scitax, http://www.scitax.com/pdf/Bulletin.55.Statistics. Reveal.Dramatic.Increase.in.SR&ED.Appeals.11-Apr-2014.pdf. See also Danny Bradbury, Canadian tech firms are getting funded, but gaps remain. *Financial Post*, February 8, 2015. http://business.financialpost.com/entrepreneur/canadian-tech-firms-are-getting-funded-but-gaps-remain

government's programme is either too complex to understand, or it does not suit the current needs of innovators."

It also discourages future applicants. This programme and the bureaucracy around it are reflective of outdated approaches to government interactions with the private sector. It's not surprising then that the World Economic Forum's World Competitiveness Report cites the number one challenge in doing business in Canada is dealing with an inefficient bureaucracy. This is an example of 21st-century red tape.

Lack of Business Skills

How important are business skills? The answer can be found in this question: Who invented the light bulb? Most people would say Thomas Edison. The right answer is Henry Woodward and Mathew Evans, two Canadians. Few people have ever heard of them. Woodward was a Toronto medical student and Evans a hotel keeper, and they invented the light bulb in 1874. Two years later they sold their patent to Thomas Edison, who improved the technology and commercialized it. He claimed it as his invention, a claim that stuck in the popular imagination. There is an important distinction between invention and innovation. Inventing the light bulb was a brilliant bit of science, but the innovation was Edison's; he perfected it, got it to market, and it formed the basis of General Electric, which grew into one of America's largest companies. Canadians are below the global average for entrepreneurial experience.[94]

94 Ipsos Report, Almost three-in-ten citizens globally say they have started a business at some point. July 22, 2022. p. 15.

This isn't the only invention that Edison is credited with that he didn't invent. The phonograph was invented by Édouard-Léon Scott de Martinville twenty years before Edison's version. And although Edison has been called "the father of motion pictures," Louis Le Prince made films years before Edison did. While Edison did invent many things, he also was able to patent and commercialize new technologies. He held 2,332 patents, some of which were his own inventions, others the uncredited inventions of others. But Edison is the only name we recognize now.

Innovation is key to future success, but there needs to be a clear path to take any new technology to market. Kevin Nilsen, President and CEO of ECO Canada, a Calgary-based environmental company, noted that, "Canada was ranked No. 1 in the world when it came to investment in clean tech innovations but we were only ranked No 16 globally when it came to generating revenue from clean tech."

While Canada is blessed with technical skills, the country lacks the commensurate entrepreneurial skills to effectively commercialize ideas. "We have a couple of key niches," Amanda Lang said. "AI is one of them. We've never been short of good ideas, and we've never been short of start-ups. Where we fell down horribly, is getting first Venture Capital angels. It's really getting our companies from Series A to any kind of meaningful size. It's at that level that we still sell out, we go south, we merge, we do a bunch of things that just don't grow our own ideas. I do think that's a level we have to work at. But I don't know what will change that because the capital is here. The capital is coming. It's more of a cultural mentality that good enough is good enough. We need to champion our businesses, make sure they know we want them to be Shopify."

A large number of students enrolling in MBA programmes are in fact engineers. While they are incredibly skilled on the engineering, operational, design and scientific aspects, they have less business management training. By completing an MBA, they are able to have both, which is needed to not only develop great ideas but also to commercialize them. But then what happens when they decide to create a start-up?

Based on the recommendation of the Barton-led Advisory Council on Economic Growth, the Canadian government created an arms-length organization called Future Skills lab, aimed at identifying and equipping Canadians with the latest skills necessary to thrive in a gig economy.

Unlike in the Western world, where the gig economy has sometimes resulted in a backlash, countries like Nigeria are finding that it offers their workers a lifeline.[95] "They would be my second god if they [could] give me even more business," said Kobo driver James Okoruwa to a local newspaper. "That's what we're praying for."

It is very difficult to grow a small Canadian business, as evidenced by the very high failure rates for those who try. There is a dearth of mentors to lead this growth. "We have only a small pool of experienced managers who can mentor the next cohort of start-ups, especially leaders who have grown companies to $100-million from $10-million."[96] According

95 Neil Munshi, Tech start-ups drive change for Nigerian truckers. *Financial Times*, August 27, 2019. https://www.ft.com/content/c6a3d1f2-c27d-11e9-a8e9-296ca66511c9

96 Gerry Remers, Canada's startup problem isn't lack of talent, but expertise in scaling up. *The Globe and Mail*, Opinion. August 31, 2016. https://www.theglobeandmail.com/report-on-business/rob-commentary/canadas-startup-problem-isnt-lack-of-alent-but-expertise-in-scaling-up/article31611569/

to another study by the Lazaridis Institute, the challenge relates to gaps in sales, marketing, and product management. And the gap is even wider. There is clearly a talent gap on the business side within Canada. "But there is also a deeper, more fundamental issue: a failure in the market for business judgement. Most of what is between an invention and a successful company is business judgement. But judgement is not for sale—a new venture cannot simply go downtown and purchase a unit of business judgement."[97]

"The upskilling piece is huge," said Jennifer Reynolds, President & CEO of Toronto Finance International. "We need to figure out what are the skills for the future. You cannot upskill your workforce until you figure out what it is you need five years from now. We are all struggling with that."

Scale

The Canadian economy is relatively small and often doesn't provide the scale needed to justify significant expenditures on R&D activities because the market "prize" is not large enough. This theme underlines many economic models, where the size of the economy is directly related to the incentive to undertake R&D. Larger economies enhance the case for R&D as it represents a larger base to spread these high fixed costs across. This is why a larger network of trade agreements

---

97 Tiff Macklem and Robert Helsley, Entrepreneurial business judgement is Canada's scarcest resource. *The Globe and Mail*, Opinion. February 6, 2017. https://www.theglobeandmail.com/report-on-business/rob-commentary/entrepreneurial-business-judgment-is-canadas-scarcest-resource/article33905688/

that provide broad access to global consumers are of greater strategic interest to a smaller country like Canada.

This is also one of the key arguments underlying the case made to grow Canada's population significantly. While scale indeed does incentivize R&D, it is by no means a necessary requirement. There are many countries much smaller than Canada that undertake far more R&D relative to GDP. Simply doubling the size of Canada's population through accelerated immigration with the same structures would not enhance Canada's R&D capacity. How then can the Canadian economy scale up so as to enhance the case to spend more on R&D?

One example could be to implement policies to help start-up and medium-sized Canadian businesses scale up, by providing them opportunities to sell to the biggest Canadian customer—the government—by ensuring they are aware of government procurement needs. Also, this is where the large Canadian players in consolidated industries like telecom, banking, health care, and insurance can keep a close eye on and ensuring they are paying attention to new Canadian technologies to give their offerings a fair shot in these markets.

6

Overcoming Protectionism, Stagnant Systems

In any bureaucracy, there's a natural tendency to let the system become an excuse for inaction.

—Chris Fussell

To become more productive and innovative, we need to look at the relative lack of competitive forces within the Canadian economy. When industries are shielded from competition, they will almost naturally become less efficient and less productive and have less market incentive to innovate. The strategic benefit of competitive dynamics is there are few, if any, other free market pressures that can directly promote and instill the urgency to innovate and remain efficient. There are few things more powerful to turn ideas into action than the feeling of a competitor's breath on your neck.

A Canadian study indicates that when Canadian manufacturers were exposed to increased U.S. competition, Canadian productivity was significantly enhanced.[98] This evidence extends to a broad cross-section of sectors and countries. Canada must shed these outdated protectionist policies. As noted by Andrei Sulzenko, "The lack of serious, sustained competitive pressures in many key sectors of the Canadian economy has made it rational for businesses to underinvest in a range of riskier innovation activities, including R&D."[99] What are the sources of this lack of competitive forces within Canada that is inhibiting innovation and productivity?

Protectionism: Restrictions on Foreign Investment and Trade

Protectionism is implicit in many Canadian policies. According to the OECD, Canada is very restrictive to foreign direct investment (FDI).[100] The most commonly used measure of how restrictive policies are with respect to allowing FDI across countries is the OECD's Foreign Direct Investment Regulatory Restrictiveness Index. This index of FDI restrictiveness measures four statutory restrictions across countries: (i) foreign equity restrictions, (ii) screening and prior approval requirements, (iii) rules for key personnel, and (iv) other restrictions on the operation of foreign enterprises. This index

---

98 A. Lileeva and D. Trefler, 2010. Improved access to foreign markets raises plant-level productivity . . . for some plants. *The Quarterly Journal of Economics, 125* (3), pp. 1051–99.

99 Andrei Sulzenko, Canada's Innovation Conundrum: Five years after the Jenkins Report, IRPP, June 2016. http://irpp.org/wp-content/uploads/2016/06/report-2016-06-09.pdf

100 OECD, FDI Regulatory Restrictiveness Index, http://www.oecd.org/investment/fdiindex.htm

is scored on a scale from 0 to 1, with 1 being the most restrictive and 0 the least. As seen in Figure 3, there are only eight countries scored by the OECD that have more restrictive FDI policies than Canada: Indonesia, Russia, China, New Zealand, India, Mexico, and Iceland. That is, Canada's FDI policies are more restrictive than all other G7 countries, and indeed among the majority of the world's most developed countries.

These restrictive FDI policies have resulted in Canada becoming less attractive to global capital. As can be seen in Figure 4, in 1980, Canada received 7 percent of the entire World's FDI stock. This has fallen steadily through the end of the 1990s. There was a turn around in the period 2000–2008, driven by the inflow of foreign

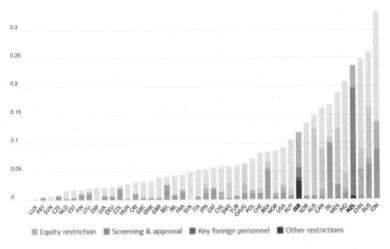

■ Equity restriction   ■ Screening & approval   ■ Key foreign personnel   ■ Other restrictions

Figure 3 Year = 2018. OECD Foreign Direct Investment Regulatory Restrictiveness Index

Source: OECD Going Digital Toolkit, based on OECD FDI Regulatory Restrictiveness Index Database, http://www.oecd.org/investment/fdiindex.htm.

Retrieved from: OECD, http://goingdigital.oecd.org/en/indicator/74

capital into Canadian resources, but this trend reversed after the 2008 global financial crisis, and the trend continues as a result of a movement away from oil and in the direction of renewables. If Canada is benchmarked against the entire EU28, the G7, or North America, a similar trend holds. These additional benchmarks are important because they reflect both the rise in emerging markets and Canada's decline within developed countries. Canada has become less attractive to FDI, and as such, is not getting all the benefits that come with FDI.

These restrictions have also resulted in lower levels of competition within Canada, lower levels of innovation, productivity, employment, and income. These restrictions have hurt the Canadian economy.

Foreign investment is important because it brings to Canada much in the way of foreign technology, managerial know how, capital, and enhanced competition, which will diffuse through the broader economy. You don't unsee a better mousetrap. It naturally inspires

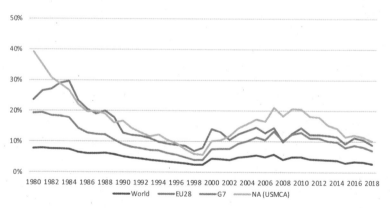

Figure 4 Canada's Shares of Inward FDI Stocks

Source: Data used to create this figure retrieved from the United Nations Conference on Trade and Development. https://unctad.org/statistics

to build something better. Short of national security considerations, there should be little restriction on foreign investment. Although some consideration should be paid to ensuring food security and access to medical goods and treatment especially in light if the vulnerabilities exposed in the COVID-19 crisis, it is still unrealistic to assume Canada can ever develop all the food, drugs, and medical supplies the country will ever need.

There is one exception to this rule that should be applied, in part, for banking and finance. In that case there is a positive externality that comes with protection that offsets the negative outcomes. This sentiment was put forward in a *National Post* article entitled "How Canada's banking protections stifle innovation at home, but give Bix Six free rein to expand abroad." RBC, Bank of Montreal, and TD are all in the midst of renewed efforts to expand in the United States.[101] "Regulation can have the side effect of pumping the brakes on innovation. A December 2017 study by the Competition Bureau noted, "there were a number of heavily regulated 'barriers' at both the federal and provincial levels that could hinder technology companies trying to enter the financial services market." [102]

But this balance must always be carefully considered. According to a 2018 C.D. Howe Report entitled *Productivity and the Financial Sector—What's Missing?*, author Jeremy Kronick finds that "Canada's

---

101 See, for example, https://www.theglobeandmail.com/business/commentary/ article-td-needs-to-keep-spending-to-build-out-its-presence-on-wall-street-if/, *The Globe and Mail*, by Andrew Willis.

102 Geoff Zochodne, How Canada's banking protections stifle innovation at home, but give Big Six free rein to expand abroad. *Financial Post*, July 23, 2018. https:// financialpost.com/news/fp-street/how-canadas-banking-protections-stifle-innovation-at-home-but-give-big-six-free-rein-to-expand-abroad

financial services sector over the last fifteen years has lagged behind other OECD countries in its contribution to productivity growth."[103] Improving productivity within the sector would enhance productivity across the entire economy because of the overall role played by the financial system.

The report also recommends changes that would better enable both fintechs and insurtechs developments within the Canadian economy. The degree and nature of regulation and protection of the Canadian banking system must be re-examined in seeking the best paths to increasing innovation and overall productivity.

Many unnecessary investment obstacles remain in the Canadian economy. First, when investments are sufficiently large and above the government's established threshold, they must go through an often opaque federal approval process and meet a "net benefit" test—that is, the investment must be shown to be "good" for Canada under the Investment Canada Act. Government decisions can be driven by true economic and national security concerns or could be perceived as protectionist in some cases. The C.D. Howe Institute and others have called for a repeal of the net benefit test. A.E. Safarian and Daniel Schwanen have written that, "The answer is that there is no good economic reason for maintaining the net-benefit test. Canada would improve its reputation and more easily attract investments if it repealed it."[104]

103 Jeremy Kronick, Productivity and the financial sector—what's missing. C.D. Howe. Commentary 508. https://cdhowe.org/sites/default/files/attachments/research_papers/mixed/Commentary_508.pdf

104 A. E. Safarian and Daniel Schwanen, There's no good economic reason for the net-benefit test. *The Globe and Mail*, May 17, 2015. https://www.theglobeandmail.com/report-on-business/economy/theres-no-good-economic-reason-for-the-net-benefit-test/article24470675/

In 2018, a Chinese state-owned enterprise bid to buy Aecon, a Canadian construction company, and was turned down. According to the government, this decision was based on security concerns. But without clear communication in all cases, there is a risk that we merely politicize security threats and they can lose their meaning. In a confused world, this is exactly the time to stick to our clear objective "rule of law" system in form and substance because it is our most valuable asset to attract investment and maintain trust in our system. Following this strategy is ultimately the best way a medium power like Canada can avoid being crushed by giants.

There is no doubt the Chinese government needs to revisit its approach to trade and investment for its next era of growth. To continue to maintain the trust of the global investment community going forward, they will need to permit additional reciprocity as well as separate private and government interests in its economy to further integrate into the global economy. As discussed in the previous chapter, an economy that is completely subservient to politics is not a recipe for enduring innovation, growth, and prosperity. As in the post–Second World War world, as everyone climbs the economic development ladder, there has to be more give-and-take so everyone can have the opportunity for mutual benefit.

The three major sectors where foreign participation is significantly restricted in Canada are telecom, air transport, and banking and finance. These three sectors are what are referred to as critical infrastructure sectors. All businesses in the economy must interact with these sectors. As a result, if they are not operating to the highest competitive global standard, their inefficiencies will be magnified across the entire economy, hurting the economy's productivity and innovation.

Telecommunications

Protectionism has resulted in lower productivity and innovation, both within the telecom sector itself and across the entire economy. Increasingly, the restrictions on foreign competition are being questioned. Increasing "over the top" technological offerings and related "cord cutting" trends are moving the market in that direction in any event.

Bold decisions must be considered to further modernize this sector and provide this essential infrastructure to the broadest and deepest pool of Canadians. In an interview with Amanda Lang, Nagib Sawaris[105] offered this perspective, "Why would you protect your own industries like they're doing here, then you need to ask yourself why isn't a Rogers in the UK, why isn't a Rogers like Vodaphone or France Telecom, why aren't they everywhere, and the answer is simple, because here they are protected. . . . They can be inefficient, and their cost structure can be expensive, as long as the consumer is paying the bill, they're fine. . . . How can you create innovation, how can you interact with other new applications and new technologies if you close yourself up?"

Many see the restrictions on foreign entry contributing to an underserved telecommunications sector where costs are high in the provision of broadband and internet services. For example, a report from the New America Foundation's Open Technology Initiative ranked Canada's voice and data rates as the highest in the world. The toll on the Canadian economy, across all sectors, is dramatic.

---

105 Amanda Lang and Kevin O'Leary Exchange, CBC. Wind Mobile's Naguib Sawiris slams Canadian Duopoly & Government. November 20, 2011. https://www.youtube.com/watch?v=-g61PnQanEg

Productivity, prosperity, and employment are all negatively impacted as a direct result of this protection.

By not interacting more, whether in the telecom sector or otherwise, the Canadian economy risks missing out on the many benefits that intense competition would bring.

Air Transport

A key component in diversifying Canada's global footprint is enhanced connectivity. There must be an increased focus on providing direct flights between business hubs. Currently, federal regulations and policy artificially restrict such connectivity. When there is demand that makes economic sense for such direct flights, then barriers to a carrier— Canadian or otherwise—to fill this demand must be eliminated. As it is, there are far too many obstacles, resulting in Canadians having to connect in busy hubs rather than flying directly to their ultimate destination, thus wasting valuable time and money. The lack of direct flights inhibits international business and reduces the competitiveness of Canadian business. It also makes the costs of deploying strategies to diversify the Canadian economy more difficult—such strategies require enhanced connectivity to new markets, an outcome inconsistent with a protected air transport industry.

For example, the two UAE carriers battled the Canadian government for years to allow for more landing rights. Granting such rights would increase Canada's connectivity to an increasingly importantly international hub. Without direct flights, thousands of Canadians can otherwise be forced to stop in Toronto, Montreal, or Europe en route, wasting time, money, and potential. This is the case for many other destinations, including India and China. Allowing foreign carriers access not only increases connectivity for Canadians and their businesses, but it also reduces prices paid, and hence increases the flow of air traffic, with the ultimate outcome of enhancing the competitiveness of the Canadian economy.

In July 2018, a high-level business delegation from the Middle East was in Calgary to discuss further collaboration between Canada and the region. One obstacle that was discussed was air links between the Middle East region and Calgary, Canada's oil capital. Houston has several daily flights to the UAE, as does Australia. In sharp contrast, Calgary has zero. All travellers on that route must transit through Toronto, Montreal, or Europe. Once again, if there is sufficient demand for a direct flight, the federal governments should not impede Canadian competitiveness and force Canadians on routes that only serve the interests of the incumbents.

Banking and Finance

Foreign participation within the Canadian banking system is also heavily restricted. However, there has been a grand bargain: the banking sector would be given protection in exchange for being heavily regulated. The banking sector has indeed delivered on the bargain in terms of providing stability.[106] It protected Canada from the Great Recession of 2008. However, it may be time to reassess some of these protections in the context of the 21st-century economy,

---

106 M. D. Bordo, A. Redish, and H. Rockoff, 2015. Why didn't Canada have a banking crisis in 2008 (or in 1930, or 1907, or . . .)? *The Economic History Review, 68* (1), pp. 218–43.

including the Bank Act. A recent *National Post* article commented, "As a result of that protection, the banks have indeed delivered stability, but they have also deployed strategies which have significantly inhibited innovation too."

While profitability is paramount, its pursuit can sometimes stifle innovation, and can come at the consumer's expense. When we deposit a cheque, banks can often hold it for three-to-five business days before the funds are available, although it takes far less than this amount of time for the cheques to be cleared. There are payment platforms in other countries that are instantaneous. But banks can benefit from holding onto those funds for several days and from other such frictions in the system. While the banks can benefit from this practice, it comes at the direct expense of customers who are forced to wait longer than necessary to access their funds.

Another tension present in the financial services industry is with the area of Open API Banking environments where individuals are able to simply make their financial data (often housed at incumbent banks) available to new entrants. This is particularly relevant to new fintech companies offering services such as wealth management, financial planning, and other innovative applications. This open banking environment has proliferated in Europe, is coming to the United States, and an expert federal advisory committee submitted a report on open banking to Chrystia Freeland, the Finance Minister that recommended the government and industry partners collaborate to design a Canadian open banking system by January 2023 but the transition has been slow.[107]

---

107 See https://www.theglobeandmail.com/business/adv/article-open-banking-is-coming-to-canada-are-our-banks-ready/

What this means is that there are obstacles to the development of fintech services in Canada—unrelated to security or privacy considerations—that may be preventing the further proliferation of innovative financial services.

As an op-ed in the *Globe and Mail* noted, "New ventures looking for customers also lament that large Canadian organizations—both public and private—are skittish about buying solutions from new companies. These issues all need to be addressed."[108] The *National Post* concurred: "More of our own innovation has to seek first customers and revenue outside Canada to make it. . . . Lately, we seem to be doing a better job of encouraging investment in Canada than we are scaling up our new innovative companies."[109] These are clear examples of how protectionism inhibits innovation.

Benefits of Liberalizing Across all Industries

The perils of protectionism can be seen in a recent study undertaken for the Canadian government.[110] The study found that if restrictions

108 Tiff Macklem and Robert Helsley, Entrepreneurial business judgement is Canada's scarcest resource. *The Globe and Mail*, Opinion. February 6, 2017. https://www.theglobeandmail.com/report-on-business/rob-commentary/entrepreneurial-business-judgment-is-canadas-scarcest-resource/article33905688/

109 Geoff Zochodne, How Canada's banking protections stifle innovation at home, but give Big Six free rein to expand abroad. *Financial Post.* July 23, 2018. https://financialpost.com/news/fp-street/how-canadas-banking-protections-stifle-innovation-at-home-but-give-big-six-free-rein-to-expand-abroad

110 W. Hejazi and D. Trefler, 2019. Implications of Canada's restrictive FDI policies on employment and productivity. *Journal of International Business Policy*, 2 (2), pp. 142–66.

on foreign investment into Canada were reduced to the average levels seen across developed countries, Canadian labour productivity would increase significantly. Such liberalization would also either raise employment by 137,400 jobs or raise annual earnings for each Canadian worker by $648, or $9.6 billion economy-wide. These results are enormous from a policy perspective. They highlight the merits of foreign investment to local economies and underscore the damage that protectionism has for the overall economy. This and other studies leave little doubt that the protectionist stance embedded in Canadian policies is damaging the innovation ecosystem in Canada and has destroyed jobs and reduced incomes.

These results are entirely consistent with the recommendations of the federal government's Red Wilson Report convened to consider government policy in an increasingly global economy over a decade ago. There was concern that Canada's economy was being hollowed out, the result of several foreign takeovers of Canadian companies. The 2008 report *Compete to Win* had several recommendations.[111] The panel recommended a reconsideration of its automatic policy review of foreign investments above a given threshold amount. It also called for allowing more foreign competition in both air transport and telecom. Despite these calls, and despite the enormous evidence of the damage protection has inflicted on the Canadian economy, successive Canadian governments have failed to act decisively on many of the recommendations.

In reviewing the progress of the Red Wilson report, The Business Council of Canada wrote, "The underlying pressures facing Canada as

---

111 Red Wilson, Compete to win, final report—June 2008. Government of Canada. https://publications.gc.ca/collections/collection_2008/ic/Iu173-1-2008E.pdf

it competes in the global economy have not abated. More than ever, we need all the advantages that a competitiveness-focused policy regime can give. The unfinished business from the Wilson panel should be a renewed priority for a country that seeks to 'compete to win.'"[112]

Import Limits on Canadians

The Canadian protectionist mindset includes our *de minimis* threshold, that is, limits on international shipments before taxes and duties are applied. An opinion published in the *Globe and Mail* was titled "Canada's customs threshold: out of step and out of pocket."[113] Citing a report by the C.D. Howe Institute, Canada's limit is among the lowest in the world, and was unchanged for decades until it was increased to C$800 but only for absences of more than 48 hours. These limits are protectionist and meant to protect domestic retailers at the expense of Canadian consumers.

The results of the C.D. Howe analysis demonstrate that "Under every scenario the authors evaluated, they have found that Canadian consumers and small businesses, as well as the federal government, all stand to benefit from even a modest increase in the threshold. Most notably, the authors highlight that it currently costs the federal

112 Business Council of Canada, Compete to win: the Wilson panel report six years later. March 2, 2015. https://thebusinesscouncil.ca/report/compete-to-win-the-wilson-panel-report-six-years-later/

113 Andrea Stairs, Canada's customs threshold: out of step and out of pocket, opinion contributed to the *Globe and Mail*, June 23, 2016. https://www.theglobeandmail.com/report-on-business/rob-commentary/canadas-customs-threshold-out-of-step-and-out-of-pocket/article30560441/

government close to $170-million to collect roughly $40-million in duties and taxes (including provincial taxes) for shipments valued between $20 and $80. Plainly stated, Canada's *de minimis* threshold is a money-losing endeavor for taxpayers." Yet despite this evidence, protectionism continues, to the detriment of the Canadian economy.

These limits are not in place to protect small retailers. To the contrary, the current *de minimis* thresholds protect larger retailers who haven't adapted to changing consumer demands. Despite the evidence demonstrating the economic benefits of lifting these limits, the protectionist mindset within Canadian government policies remains detrimental to innovation and productivity. What better ways to incentivize large retailers to update their business models than to expose them to international competition?

Supply Management

In order to guarantee farmers a stable income, the government implemented Supply Management, a system of tariffs and quotas that raises the prices that Canadians pay for cheese and dairy, eggs, and poultry, and protects the industry from foreign competition. Dairy tariffs are nearly 300 percent for butter and cream, and 240 percent for cheese, whole milk, and yogurt. As a result, farmers benefit, but productivity and innovation are impeded, and consumers are hurt.

There remain significant quotas that limit the variety of cheese Canadians can eat—once those quotas are exhausted, Canadians are forced to eat Canadian cheese. We are not saying this is a bad outcome in and of itself, but strategies must be deployed that allow Canadians to eat the cheese of their choice, not what is dictated by government policies. This policy has a significantly larger impact on the poor, who have difficulty paying the higher prices that result from protection. It's remarkable how much cheaper cheese and dairy products are in the United States, and how the government has protected this industry to the detriment of Canadians.

Inter-provincial Trade

At the meeting of provincial premiers in July 2018, there was an agreement to allow more inter-provincial trade in beer and wine. Christy Clark, former Premier of British Columbia, said, "It's ridiculous. We are in the midst of a trade war . . . and at the same time we can't trade with one another." Clarke said the inability of provinces to trade with one another is self-defeating and was President Trump's greatest "weapon against us" in trade battles.[114]

The barriers to trade between Canadian provinces reflect a backward-looking protectionist view. As noted in a recent Senate report, under Canada's free trade agreement with Europe, "European companies have easier access to some Canadian markets than Canadian companies from another province."[115] The economic impacts of these barriers are potentially huge, potentially more than $100 billion in lost prosperity.

---

114 Christy Clark, Free trade within Canada | Premiers' League, CBC News, July 20, 2018. https://www.youtube.com/watch?v=SAYfBFtjAUI&app=desktop

115 Trevor Tombe, Why barriers to trade between the provinces leave us all poorer. Maclean's. June 15, 2016. https://www.macleans.ca/economy/economicanalysis/why-barriers-to-trade-between-the-provinces-leave-us-all-poorer/

A Poorly Developed Canadian Ecosystem

Another hurdle is the lack of a frictionless platform that allows Canadians to pursue their passions and create great businesses. "Overregulation and excessive taxation are both major deterrents to innovation. We regulate our banks, we regulate telecoms, our aerospace industry, agriculture, our power /energy . . . we regulate everything! Canada's regulatory landscape stifles innovation through protectionism and creation of oligopolistic markets. In a nutshell we often kill competitive environments that typically allow innovation to thrive!"[116]

Dominic Barton concurred. "We have to think about that in our regulatory framework, how many regulations we have, how long it takes to get things done," he said. "We have got to simplify and reduce that significantly. Canada should be one of the easiest, fastest places to build a business."

Michael G. Helander graduated with a PhD from the University of Toronto and with two co-founders started a company called OTI Lumionics Inc. As a student, he published more than 100 articles and secured 4 patents. His start-up relates to the Fourth Industrial Revolution where he developed a process that "could eliminate 70% of the manufacturing steps, reduce costs by up to 50%, and could improve performance by two to three times."[117] More fundamentally, he describes how his innovation in manufacturing would disrupt the industry—rather than building multi-billion-dollar factories, his approach requires up-front costs that are 100 times smaller, thus

116 Rotman Executive MBA student, essay submission.
117 Presentation at the Rotman School of Management.

enabling the distribution of production facilities around the world rather than concentrated in one location.

Helander spoke of the many challenges his start-up faced. In a talk at the Rotman School of Management, he talked about the interest to buy his technology exhibited by Asians, Americans, and Europeans. "If we are to take all this innovation developed here in Canada and sell it off to a foreign company, half-way across the world, they won't do anything in Canada. Rather than do that, we decided to open our own company. As a Canadian, we had this conservative view. This is Canada, we don't do advanced manufacturing here, and we don't invest in new technologies because it's risky. We can make auto parts, we can dig oil out of the ground, and we can chop down trees." He spoke of how he was encouraged to move his operations to China, the United States, or South Korea. As someone once said to him, "What do Canadians know about opening an advanced manufacturing facility?"

The path of a start-up is not easy. Helander struggled for almost three years and couldn't raise capital or find supporters. This changed when he became part of the Rotman School of Management's Creative Destruction Lab (CDL) at the University of Toronto. The CDL is an example of an ecosystem that is needed throughout Canada—not just at the University of Toronto. The thinking, culture, and ecosystem that is the CDL must permeate the business and entrepreneurial culture throughout the country. As part of the CDL, Helander was able to tap into the knowledge, networks, and, most importantly, the "market for judgement" of thought leaders from the business community. Throughout this process, Helander received mentorship and funding, both of which were critical. Helander's company is now a success, attributable in large part to being part of the CDL.

The CDL represents a frictionless ecosystem with all of the key ingredients needed to develop, commercialize, and scale ventures. Without access to this, the company may have very likely moved to another country, to the detriment of Canada. The CDL has now spread across the country and is increasingly undertaking activities globally. In addition, we have the Toronto Metropolitan University's Digital Media Zone, which is a world-class incubator. We need to double down on these strategies. It is exactly this kind of thinking and approach to start-ups and to innovation that must be proliferated across the country.

Superclusters

The Canadian government earmarked nearly $1 billion to create five superclusters, or "Global Innovation Clusters" that would see stakeholders agglomerate to create an ecosystem that enables innovation. The initiative involves investments into existing, successful clusters and scale them up to become superclusters.[118]

This initiative is a first of its kind for Canada, fostering stronger connections—from large anchor firms to start-ups, from post-secondary institutions to research and government partners—and opening the door to new forms of industry partnerships. It represents a significant commitment to partnering with industry and supporting the success of leading domestic and global companies that choose to innovate in Canada.

---

118 Government of Canada, About Canada's global innovation clusters. https://ised-isde.canada.ca/site/global-innovation-clusters/en/about-canadas-innovation-clusters-initiative

We believe this to be an interesting initiative with the potential to allow start-ups in to better network and work with other stakeholders and commercialize and scale in Canada.

But there's a challenge with the government undertaking such an initiative without addressing the underlying barriers to innovation. The supercluster initiative could hit a brick wall if the incumbents across the regulated and protected industries continue to cling to legacy systems and resist innovation, and if government bureaucracy continues to smother by, for example administering R&D credits by CRA auditors. And this list goes on. Therefore, while the supercluster initiative is potentially useful, it is not a substitute for the bold changes necessary to allow Canada to achieve its potential.

Government must face these obstacles head on. A start-up that gets all the ingredients within a supercluster will fail if it can't get a customer. It's relatively easy to allocate a billion dollars to superclusters. But it takes bold leadership to address the real obstacles, especially if it means undermining the position of incumbents in protected industries. It is the time for bold leadership.

7

From Industry to the Individual: The New Economy—Powered by the People

To be complex does not mean to be fragmented. This is the paradox and the genius of our Canadian civilization.

—Adrienne Clarkson

Waiting for big industry to open a big car plant or expand an oil sands project doesn't look like a good bet in today's world, but betting on individual Canadians to put themselves and others to work has always paid off. An updated plan on how to do this also plays to our strengths and heritage. As a country of immigrants, many of whom came with nothing but a dream to make the most of the Canadian promise is what built our country. But how we rediscover that spirit and reinvent it for the modern economy often seems out of reach. A recent poll found, since 2018, entrepreneurship has increased most among women, Gen Z/Millennials, those with a lower income level and those with a lower or middle education.[119]

119 See Ipsos Report, July 22, 2022.

"All over the rich world, new businesses are springing to life", reads the title of an Economist article.[120] They show that the number of new enterprises in the fourth quarter of 2021 was 15 percent higher than pre-pandemic, translating into about a million new businesses springing up across the OECD. "More entrepreneurship is likely to be good for the economy. New businesses try out fresh ideas and ways of doing things, while drawing capital and people away from firms that are stuck in their ways", the article reads.

Here's what we know: small business still represents and employs more than 70 percent of Canadians. It remains the lifeblood of our economy, but the old economy is in transition to the digital economy and it will leave many behind. As the pressures of the COVID-19 crisis have shown, this will only get worse if we don't adapt quickly. This is most apparent in the restaurant and hotel industry, which were hit very hard. We need to find ways to allow Canadians to reinvent themselves and tap into their talents, experience, and energy to unlock their future potential. Everyone has learned something or some skill that can be repackaged and redeployed into the modern economy for value. Who doesn't have something they can offer the market? In the United States, self-employment numbers rebounded better than payroll employment, and it was also reflected in the number of people who applied for tax identification numbers, which surged by 77 percent in the third quarter of 2020 and is often an indicator of people starting a new business. The COVID-19 pandemic unleashed a wave of start-ups across the world. For example, in the United States, start-ups rose by 82 percent in the third quarter of 2020 compared to the same quarter in 2019. There are similar trends

---

120 See https://www.economist.com/finance-and-economics/2022/04/23/all-over-the-rich-world-new-businesses-are-springing-to-life

in the United Kingdom, France, Germany, and Japan. Worldwide, 3 in 10 entrepreneurs, who started a business over the last two years, were motivated by the pandemic.[121] In Canada, two million of us started a business during the pandemic. In the post-COVID-19 world, there is renewed opportunity for Canadian exporters. "The Canada brand might have more value than it did a year ago," said Douglas Kennedy, RBC managing director at the Centre for Global Enterprise at York University because of factors like reliability in trade relations, rule of law, cultural openness, and high product safety standards.[122]

One of the critical keys to future success is *a skilled and empowered workforce*. It isn't wise to close the doors to immigration because that would jeopardize the Canada to be enjoyed in retirement. Canada needs new workers to pay for the hospitals and pensions deserve and expect to enjoy after a lifetime of contributions. Immigration is absolutely necessary to support our retirement promise and to ensure a growing and diverse labour force. With the exception of Canada's indigenous peoples, Canada is a country of immigrants. And like many Western countries, Canada's low birth rates would result in a falling population were it not for immigration.

In 1967, Canada admitted 222,900 immigrants. As seen in Figure 5, Canada's immigration numbers have fluctuated widely since, hitting an all-time low of 84,300 in 1985, but rising sharply to 256,600 in 1993. Since 2005, Canada has been admitting around 250,000 immigrants per year. Over time, the number of foreign-born Canadians has increased. As seen in Figure 6, in 1961, there were 2,844,263

---

121 See Ipsos Report, July 22, 2022.
122 See https://www.theglobeandmail.com/featured-reports/article-k-shaped-recovery-provides-opportunities-for-some-canadian-exporters/

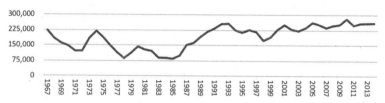

Figure 5 Canadian Immigration, 1967 to present

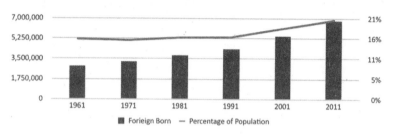

Figure 6 Canada's Foreign-Born Population, Numbers, and Percentage of Population

Source: Statistics Canada. 150 Years of Immigration. http://www.statcan.gc.ca/pub/11-630-x/11-630-x2016006-eng.htm

foreign-born Canadians in Canada, or 15.6 percent of the population. By 1991, this number had increased to 4,342,890, or 16.1 percent of the population. In 2011, there were 6,775,770, constituting 20.6 percent of the population. In the United States, the immigrant population is 14.4 percent.

Canada's Increased Diversity

The sources of immigration have changed significantly over Canada's history, creating greater diversity. A century ago, it was French and British who moved to Canada. At the turn of the 20th century, Prime Minister Wilfrid Laurier wanted to populate the empty prairies and sent out brochures and agents, trying to recruit farmers from Britain, the United States, Germany, and the Scandinavian countries. When this didn't attract enough potential farmers, he widened the search to Eastern Europe, though some members of the government were reluctant. The immigrants who arrived started the agricultural economy, which would prove to be lucrative and lasting. Today, immigrants to Canada come from everywhere. As reflected in Figure 7, there has been a rise in the share of immigrants coming from Asia, the Middle East, and North Africa. There is much evidence to demonstrate that increased diversity brings not only social benefits but financial benefits as well, the so-called "Diversity Dividend."[123]

A great example of this diversity dividend was noted by Microsoft's former CEO, Steve Ballmer, on why Microsoft chose Richmond, B.C. to open a development centre. It was "for one reason only—Canada happens to be more open to people from around the world" than the United States or other countries. The centre would employ researchers from 40 countries. "Where else would you bring people [from around the world] and have them mix comfortably," he said.[124]

"I think one of the things that sets us apart," said Amanda Lang, "is in the world of populism and territorialism we are an immigrant nation. We will continue to bear the fruit of that. The values that allow for immigrants to want to come to Canada and then do well when they arrive are very subtle, but they are pervasive, and they influence all of us.

---

123 Bessma Momani and Jillian Stirk, Diversity dividend: Canada's global advantage, centre for international governance. 2017. https://www.cigionline.org/static/documents/documents/DiversitySpecial%20Report%20WEB_0.pdf

124 Konrad Yakabuski, As sun sets on Vista, Ballmer looks "into the Cloud'." *The Globe and Mail*, October 22, 2009. www.theglobeandmail.com/report-on-business/as-sun-sets-on-vista-ballmer-looks-into-the-clouds/article1203786/

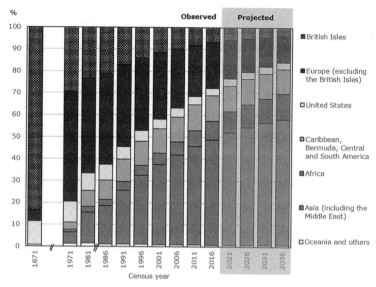

Note: // refers to a break in the time series.
Sources: Statistics Canada, Census of Population, 1871 to 2006, 2016; National Household Survey, 2011; Immigration and Diversity: Population Projections for Canada and its Regions, 2011 to 2036 (reference scenario).

Figure 7 Distribution of foreign-born population, by region of birth, Canada, 1871 to 2036

Retrieved from: https://www.statcan.gc.ca/en/dai/btd/othervisuals/other009

They make all of us think differently and live differently. While it's not necessarily a stated goal, we will be more inclusive, we will understand other cultures and points of view. That's who we are as a people."

Canadian support for immigration continues to increase. A poll released in 2022 by the Environics Institute for Survey Research find that support for immigration in Canada has doubled over the past 45 years. While just 35 percent of those surveyed in 1977 were in support of immigration levels, that number has increased to 69 percent in 2022.[125]

125 https://www.theglobeandmail.com/canada/article-canadians-more-supportive-than-ever-of-immigration-new-poll-finds-but/

There are other benefits—immigrants tend to be more entrepreneurial than those born in Canada.[126] "There is a much higher level of entrepreneurship within recent immigrant populations than the native population because those who come here are in an environment and context where they are trying desperately to succeed and working hard to make their way," said Jean Charest.

Many of the world's largest companies were founded by immigrants. "About 40 percent of Fortune 500 companies were founded either by immigrants, or by the sons and daughters of immigrants. Companies like AT&T, IBM, Coca-Cola, Microsoft, McDonald's, Goldman Sachs, eBay, Kohls, Comcast, Pfizer, Yahoo!, and many others were all founded by immigrants or their children."[127] One study found that immigrants started more than half of all billion-dollar start-ups, and that immigrants made up 70 percent of key management roles in those companies.[128]

Similar evidence exists for Canada. The Labour Force Survey reports that the tendency for immigrants to be entrepreneurs (self-employed) is much higher than for those born in Canada.[129] Fifty percent of Canadian restaurants are run by immigrants. We do not

126 Cillian O'Brien, Immigrant-owned firms create more jobs than those with Canadian-born owners: StatCan. CTVNews.ca, April 24, 2019. beta.ctvnews.ca/national/business/2019/4/24/1_4393134.html

127 https://www.theatlantic.com/news/archive/2017/01/companies-against-trumps-ban/515028/

128 Weston Phippen, The CEOs revolting against Trump's travel ban. *The Atlantic*, January 30, 2017. HTTPS://WWW.THEATLANTIC.COM/NEWS/ARCHIVE/2017/01/COMPANIES-AGAINST-TRUMPS-BAN/515028/

129 Statistics Canada, Economic insights: Business ownership and employment in immigrant-owned firms in Canada. https://www150.statcan.gc.ca/n1/pub/11-626-x/11-626-x2016057-eng.htm#n2

know where the next generation of history-altering innovations will come from. It was an immigrant, Sergey Brin, who co-founded Google, and Steve Jobs, the son of a Syrian immigrant, who co-founded Apple. These companies were not formed by members of dynasties past such as the Rockefellers, Vanderbilts, or Kennedys. It often takes hungry "outsiders" to reimagine a future less tethered to the past. Countries close their immigration doors at their own peril. Immigration brings energy, new ideas, and fresh initiatives. There is an entrenched idea that immigrants take jobs from existing Canadians, but the evidence demonstrates the opposite; immigrants create jobs. They often put themselves and others to work.

"One advantage that Canada starts with—and it's imperative on us to maintain—is a sense of inclusion," said Laura McGee, CEO of Diversio. "It's a real baked-in cultural commitment to diversity and the belief that it truly is our strength. It brings motivation, helps us move more quickly and identify new market opportunities. Remaining self-aware, self-reflective around the fact that that is an advantage and how we maintain that and in fact grow that advantage is the single biggest thing that we could do to stay competitive."

Another aspect of diversity is the gender gap in C-suites and boards, one that Camilla Sutton tracks closely as president and CEO of Women in Capital Markets. A former head of Scotiabank's global FX business, Sutton said Canada has a perception gap. "The average Canadian probably feels like there's a lot of talk about diversity (and) there's a ton written about women on boards," she said. "We are seeing more females in position to take on CEO roles. But the numbers are still stuck. Only 4 percent of Canadian TSX companies have a female as CEO."

Sutton said Canada is "mid-path" in gender diversity on the global scale. "We have more work to do. We continue to see slow change. We need something to occur. We need a shock to the system to create real change. I suspect what we get is the slow-paced change. It's more conservative and more palatable to the average Canadian." And change can't come fast enough for John Ruffolo, Founder & Managing Partner, Maverix Private Equity, who stated "I believe that we are missing opportunities where women see things very differently from men and women are the biggest buyers of consumer goods. We didn't have any women on the investing team, shame on us, we are losing out."

Canada attracts immigrants, which benefits companies, both Canadian and international, that are looking to grow their global businesses. Michael Tamblyn, chief executive at Rakuten Kobo, says that he gets to draw from the diversity of Canada's population and "bring all of that experience of other cultures and other countries into our offices in Toronto. We don't have to reach too far to find people who have grown up in countries all over the world who can give us insights into how those countries operate as markets, operate as cultures, the local traditions. That is a huge benefit when you're trying to run an international business from Toronto."

Kobo was founded by Canadian bookstore chain Indigo Books & Music Inc and spun off as a separate entity, with Indigo retaining majority interest. In 2011, Kobo agreed to be sold to Rakuten, a Japanese technology company. Rakuten Kobo, which is the world's second-biggest e-book company and trails only Amazon, is run out of Toronto.

Technological advances, digital devices, and internet access have enabled Canadians to work increasingly from home and coworking places, eliminating the need for traditional office spaces and opening up opportunities that are not limited by location, according to a CBC report.[130]

There is no question that Canada will always be a destination for those looking for a better life. However, those with entrepreneurial aspirations may go elsewhere. The most talented immigrants have many options and will emigrate to the country that offers the greatest opportunities. There is also evidence that, even if immigrants come to Canada, some of the most talented leave to more innovative and prosperous countries when the opportunity arises—often within their first year.

Canada has an opportunity to attract talent at a time when the social and political climate in other countries is less welcoming. "We were getting amazing candidates to come here because of the political climate and the openness of Canada," said John Ferguson, president and CEO of Canadian freight and logistics services provider Purolator. "These candidates were much more attracted to the climate in Canada than the US. Despite some of the issues around currency or cost-of-living, there was a real attraction to the type of social values that we have here."

However, protectionist policies, which limit immigrants from practising their profession within Canada, will also deter many skilled immigrants. Average incomes in Canada are significantly lower when immigrants are not able to practise their trade—not just the incomes of the immigrants, but the average for all Canadians. These restrictive policies also negatively impact Canada's innovative

---

130 Don Pittis, Led by the tech sector, Canadians are working around the world while staying home. CBC News, September 9, 2019. www.cbc.ca/news/business/employment-remote-work-1.5269792

ecosystem significantly. As such, credentialing (a provincial mandate) must be addressed as a way to both attract top talent and ensure talent is fully utilized. The obstacles to skilled immigrants to work in their areas of expertise is not in Canada's economic interest and simply works to protect special interests. This mindset comes at a significant cost.

Why would a skilled medical professional decide to come to Canada—where we need more doctors—if there are unnecessary obstacles to practising their trade? An immigrant would certainly prefer a country more welcoming of their skills. It may be that immigrants who still choose to come to Canada, despite such restrictions, are likely the ones with fewer options. This speaks to an important sample selection of the immigrants Canada is attracting. Allowing immigrants and foreign trained professionals to participate fully in the Canadian economy must be addressed across the spectrum, and is now a pressing issue with nursing with the fallout from post-pandemic health care worker capacity and burnout.

The most common reason given to immigrants who can't work in their field is that they don't have Relevant Canadian Experience (RCE). If Canadian companies had more interest in penetrating fast-growing emerging markets, they would find more value in hiring these skilled immigrants. Removing unnecessary protectionist policies, while still maintaining general professional standards, would accomplish that.

Why did Elon Musk, who spent time at Queen's University in Kingston, Ontario, decide not to build his business in Canada? "We don't spend enough time looking at the people who leave," C.D. Howe's William B.P. Robson said. "We lose about 70,000 people a year. And the people whom we lose tend to be highly educated, they tend to be high earners. Some of them are people who arrived in

Canada and decided to leave. We're better off that they were here at all. But we should be thinking about that emigration."

The *Globe and Mail's* Doug Sanders points out that most of Canada's modern history consists not of immigration into our country, but the exodus of those who went elsewhere. The United States has been the main beneficiary of this.

One of Canada's leading fintech start-ups was frustrated by many of the best people are simply going to Silicon Valley—the salaries, stock options, and opportunities are just too attractive to give up. A much smaller fintech with just four programmers had the same problem, with one of their programmers leaving for Silicon Valley to earn a salary that was 50 percent higher, and in U.S. dollars.

"It makes it so that, if one country is not performing as well as another country, people are going to the one that is performing better—competitive governance is what I'm calling it, Tim Draper, a venture capitalist at the Silicon Valley firm Draper Fisher Jurvetson and one of Estonia's leading tech boosters, said."[131]

Notwithstanding the issues of sample selection discussed above, for decades, people have overcome major obstacles and embraced significant risks to make their way to Canada. These are brave people seeking new opportunities for themselves and their families, often sacrificing tremendously for their children. It would be difficult to argue that these newcomers are risk-averse. Why is it that Canadians, including the large number of immigrants who have joined the Canadian family over the past fifty years, continue to behave as if they are risk-averse?

---

131 *The Best American Travel Writing* 2018 edited by Cheryl Strayed, Jason Wilson page 145.

There are two possible hypotheses to explain this phenomenon. The first is that entrepreneurial immigrants are unable to implement their innovative ideas, stifled by conservative Canadian institutions and government regulations. This was a theme that ran through many of our interviews with immigrants. An alternative hypothesis is that those people who decide to come to Canada are like Canadians before them: risk-averse. The risk-seeking immigrants go to the United States or other countries with less government bureaucracy, and where it is easier to access credit. The answer is likely a combination of the two, but the impact that conservative institutions in stifling innovation and entrepreneurial endeavours cannot be understated.

C.D. Howe's William B.P. Robson said, "We've tended to take for granted that people would come to Canada because it was such a great place. Of course, it is a good place. But the contrast between the opportunities here and many of the countries that provide immigrants to Canada is going to shrink over time. Many of these countries are raising their living standards rapidly. They have high investment rates. Many of them have become politically more stable and attractive as places to live and raise a family. So Canada needs to think about competition for people—increasing its attractiveness to talent."

Before Canada ramps up its immigration levels, it must first aggressively embrace bold policies to enhance its innovation ecosystem. Higher immigration levels without major steps to improve Canada's innovative capacity would just expand our innovation challenges. Enhancing Canada's innovation capacity would result in the arrival of the very best talent possible and would deliver magnified growth and prosperity for Canada.

An important dimension to both attracting and retaining top talent is compensation. Salaries need to compare on a global scale. In an environment where there is tremendous protection for Canadian companies from foreign competition, there is little need to worry about global rivals. Banks, telecoms, airlines, and, to a lesser extent, large retailers. simply compete with other Canadian firms. They strive to be the best in Canada. We need to change this mindset—these companies must strive to be the best in the world. That requires the very best talent, and to attract that talent, Canadian salaries must be globally competitive. Andre Bach, a Rotman MBA student, said, "raising the salaries for quality talent to be on par with global wages that are being paid for similar top roles south of the border and around the world would prevent the brain drain from happening."

Optimizing on Internal Labour Flows

The pipeline of talent must come from both inside Canada's borders and through immigration. To maximize the internal pipeline, Canada must have a world-class educational system, so as to optimize on the resources within Canada's borders.

Since 1970, the demand for skills that can be considered routine has persistently fallen, whereas the demand for those skills that involve non-routine analytical or interpersonal interactions have increased. These trends are reflected in Figure 8. Those who are digitally literate are much more likely to be employed, receive higher wages, have good to excellent health, have high levels of political efficacy, and high levels of trust (OECD). According to the Canadian Chamber of Commerce's *Canada's Top 10 Barriers to Competitiveness in 2016*, "Poor Literacy, numeracy and digital skills" impede productivity within the Canadian workforce.

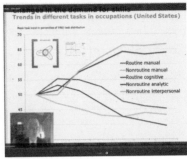

Figure 8 The importance of digital skills

Source: Presentation made at the Rotman School of Management.

When asked whether they see the need for change in the curriculum, school board officials identified a need for enhancing critical thinking skills, programming skills, soft skills, and life skills, which need to include skills in entrepreneurship. When asked what the main obstacles within the educational system are, the answer was surprising. We assumed it would be a lack of financial resources. But this wasn't the case—the resources are available. Rather, it was resistance to change on the part of teachers.

There are also significant gaps in how well students are prepared for the enormous transition to post-secondary education and a general lack of life skills. High school graduation rates are rising (over 80 percent in Ontario), yet students don't feel they are prepared for post-secondary education or life on their own.[132] Clearly, educational systems must better prepare students for the transition to university,

132 Students feel unprepared for university life. CBC News, March 08, 2011. https://www.cbc.ca/news/canada/ottawa/students-feel-unprepared-for-university-life-1.1114699

but also focus on the development of skills that drive prosperity in a 21st-century economy that may not require a university degree. We must be more open to skills and vocational training that provides both value to the economy and a meaningful career path for Canadians.

Indigenous Canadians Are an Important Source of Talent

In order for Canada to optimize its potential, there must also be a much more serious effort to engage with Canada's indigenous communities. Numbering almost two million, or 5 percent of Canada's population, this represents a significant potential additional engine of Canadian prosperity. On average, incomes per person are about one half that of the broader Canadian population. If effective strategies are put in place to close this gap, this would add $50 billion of GDP to the Canadian economy. This would empower Indigenous communities and promote economic reconciliation.

Sharleen Gale, chair of the First Nations Major Projects Coalition, wrote, "For generations, First Nations communities have been constrained by the Indian Act and decades of government paternalism and over-regulation. We did not have the chance to break into the modern economy, and lacked the basic business tools available to other Canadians. We could not borrow money to buy and build our homes, let alone get the funds needed to make major investments."[133]

133 Walid Hejazi, How Canada can, and must, empower Indigenous communities: U of T expert. October 01, 2018. https://www.utoronto.ca/news/how-canada-can-and-must-empower-indigenous-communities-u-t-expert

There must be new approaches to engage Indigenous communities and to remove systemic barriers to their engagement with the modern economy. Municipalities have recurring revenues year over year from their tax base and are able to issue municipal bonds that are backed by provincial governments. Down the road from these municipalities are Indigenous communities that have neither—they do not have property taxes as a recurring revenue source, and the federal legislation explicitly states that the federal government will not guarantee Indigenous bond issues. Unlike municipalities, Indigenous communities are unable to fund infrastructure and other needed investments.

One proposal put forth at the 2017–2018 CanInfra[134] competition was entitled The Indigenous Infrastructure Investment Trust (3IT), which is a framework that would put Indigenous communities on an equal footing with municipalities. This would allow for the mobilization of capital into Indigenous communities in a way that would enable the development of local infrastructure. This approach has proliferated across the developing world as reflected in a recent World Bank report and can easily work in the context of Canada's Indigenous communities.[135] This would enable talent from the Indigenous communities to participate fully in the Canadian economy.

134 CanInfra Challenge. https://www.caninfra.ca/ and https://www.caninfra.ca/indigenous-infrastructure-investment-trust-3it

135 Mobilizing Islamic Finance for Infrastructure Public-Private Partnerships, The World Bank, 2017. https://documents1.worldbank.org/curated/en/898871513144724493/pdf/122039-WP-P159471-12-12-2017-11-42-45-MobilizingIslamicFinancefor InfrastructurePPPsFINAL.pdf

The Migration of Labour to Cities

Migration of human populations is a central theme of the 21st century. In his book *Arrival City, Globe and Mail* columnist Doug Saunders wrote, "What will be remembered about the twenty-first century, more than anything else except perhaps the effects of a changing climate, is the great, and final shift of human populations out of rural, agricultural life and into cities. We will end this century as wholly urban species."[136]

Among the first waves of immigrants more than a century ago were farmers. Some weren't farmers by choice, but came to Canada to take advantage of the free land that was on offer—160 acres. Far more land than they could ever hope to own in the old country, whichever that old country was. But now immigrants come to the cities: Toronto, Vancouver, Calgary, Montreal. And it isn't just those from other countries; the lure of the big city continues to draw Canadians from rural communities, as it always has. Saunders argues that the great migration of humans is creating a special kind of urban space. "These transitional spaces—arrival cities—are the places where the next great economic and cultural boom will be born, or where the next great explosion of violence will occur. The difference depends on our ability to notice, and our willingness to engage."[137]

Saunders reports that many of the residents of Toronto's Thorncliffe Park are from the Indian subcontinent and hope to start a small business at some point. They are engaged in programmes

136 Doug Saunders, *Arrival City: The Final Migration and Our Next World.* Vintage Books Canada, 2011. p. 1.
137 Saunders, p. 3.

that teach them English, bookkeeping and inventory, licensing, and incorporation. If the neighbourhood is looked at solely in terms of numbers, it is an impoverished ghetto—one study had family incomes averaging $20,000 a year. Yet, in other ways, Thorncliffe Park is a success. There are few vacancies, and it operates successfully as a way station, a way for those who came from rural villages to adapt to both a foreign country and a new urban reality. These Arrival Cities, as Saunders calls them, are crucial. These people "have an amazingly consistent record of entering the middle-class urban mainstream within a generation."[138] The neighbourhood seems perpetually poor, but that is because residents are leaving and graduating into the middle class, replaced by immigrants who have arrived with very little. The ongoing poverty is actually a signal of success. Toronto has what Saunders characterized as the most complete collection of Arrival Cities in the world. The city takes in 40 percent of the country's immigrants.

Canada's history proves that immigration has worked to create one of the most peaceful and prosperous nations in the world where many can come and work as one. However, with the world and competition for talent becoming more competitive, we need to also become more aggressive and bold in making sure we have an immigration policy for the 21st century.

---

138 Saunders, p. 314.

8

Gridlock

Be not afraid of going slowly, be afraid only of standing still.

—Chinese proverb

Canada's physical infrastructure gap extends far beyond pipelines and the digital tools needed to better integrate Canada into the global economy. A 2017 Canada Chamber of Commerce study[139] "found that congestion in Toronto, Vancouver and Montreal is responsible for adding nearly 88 million hours annually to Canadians' commutes. That is over 10,000 years' worth of extra time every year that drivers in those cities are stuck in their vehicles." Toronto, Vancouver, and Montreal routinely show up in the top ten worst traffic cities in the world. This tends to be a revolving list, depending on criteria, but on occasion Toronto has beaten out all-time champion Los Angeles for

---

139 Canadian Chamber of Commerce, Canadian problems that infrastructure investment can solve. July 2017. Summary provided here: https://www.pppcouncil. ca/web/P3_Knowledge_Centre/Research/Stuck_in_Traffic_for_10_000_ years__Canadian_Problems_that_Infrastructure_Investment_Can_Solve.aspx?WebsiteKey= 712ad751-6689-4d4a-aa17-e9f993740a89

the number one spot. The city's Don Valley Parkway was built to carry 60,000 vehicles per day, and now handles more than 100,000. The 401 Highway is the busiest in North America.

More than 80 percent of Canadians now live in urban areas, and traffic will likely get worse before it gets better. But it is imperative that it get better. Toronto's Chamber of Commerce listed traffic congestion as the single biggest drag on the local economy, costing up to $11 billion in lost productivity and other costs. Those other costs associated with gridlock are harder to measure, but they are significant. Long commutes are linked to anxiety, stress, obesity, and divorce (Swedish researchers found that couples who commuted more than 45 minutes were far more likely to break up).

Traffic congestion isn't a modern phenomenon. Two thousand years ago, Julius Caesar banned chariots during daytime hours in Rome to relieve congestion. In 1879, New York had a five-hour horse-drawn carriage traffic jam. But the modern version has scaled up; in 2010, Beijing had a twelve-day, 100-kilometre traffic jam, and it isn't China's most congested city. From 2012 to 2015, Chinese police reported 104 million road rage incidents.

One of the reasons we find ourselves in such a mess, commuter-wise, has to do with government investment in infrastructure. Between 1955 and 1977, investment in Canadian infrastructure, including public transit, grew at a healthy 4.8 percent annually, keeping pace with both population growth and urbanization. But between 1977 and 2001, that figure was only 0.1 percent. The Federation of Canadian Municipalities estimates the urban transit and transportation deficit is more than $45 billion.

Commuting by car is time-consuming, frustrating, carbon-intensive, expensive, and soul destroying. Unfortunately, public transit is often worse; the clogged roads and angry, distracted drivers still make for a better experience. Only 12 percent of Canadian commuters take public transit to work.

Political expediency has been a long-running curse. Plans are made to seduce voters, then scrapped by the next administration. No one wants to spend the money (sometimes by raising taxes) and start something that won't be finished for eight years—just in time for the next government to bask in its success. The view among urban geographers is that things have to get unbearable before they get better. But they are getting unbearable. In Los Angeles, voters approved a $120 billion tax over the next 40 years that would be devoted entirely to transit. Decades of smog and gridlock on its congested highways had finally worn them down. The key was that the tax money raised would go exclusively to public transit.[140] London's congestion tax has broad support from citizens, as does a similar tax in Stockholm and Milan. There is hope for infrastructure spending in Canada. Prime Minister Trudeau initially committed $32 billion to infrastructure spending, then added another $60 billion.

Governments bear a lot of the blame for congestion, but commuters aren't blameless. Human behaviour is a factor. We tend to over-estimate our abilities as drivers. We slow down to look at accidents, drive while texting or eating breakfast. The bigger the vehicle, the safer we feel, and the more aggressively we drive.

What if we took human behaviour out of the equation? We are on the cusp of the era of autonomous vehicles (AVs) that make informed decisions on their own. The birth of the AVs can be traced to 2004 and

140 https://www.latimes.com/opinion/livable-city/la-ol-metro-elkind-measure-m-transit-waste-20170317-story.html

a 230-kilometre race that was sponsored by the U.S. Department of Defense. Fifteen vehicles that had been modified to drive by themselves were pitted against one another in the Mojave Desert. First prize was $1 million. The farthest any of the cars got was 11.78 kilometres before crashing, breaking down, stalling, or failing into a gully.

The following year the prize money was doubled to $2 million and five vehicles finished the course. The winner was built by a group at Stanford University, and Google immediately hired them to start developing its own AV. By 2010, there was a working prototype. Now Google's fleet of AVs have logged more than a million test miles. Most car manufacturers have an AV, either as prototype or in the design stage. Uber intends to be driverless by 2030. Both Apple and Blackberry are developing an AV. Cities like San Francisco and Malmö, Sweden, have AVs navigating their streets to gauge their safety and effectiveness.

The City of Toronto's Transportation Services Division estimated that AVs would result in a 90 percent drop in traffic fatalities and will ease congestion. AVs would always be moving at an optimum speed and taking the best route, using continuous information. The City of Toronto estimated $6 billion in annual savings, which would result from the deployment of AVs.

This is only if most AVs are shared, however. And AVs could expand on what we feel is a viable commute, which might put more cars on the road. If we're prepared to drive 60 kilometres through paralysed angry traffic, how far would we go if we could sleep or work during that time?

The future of transportation will likely bring some relief to our congested roads. But we won't know how until it happens. Fifty years ago, there was a Canadian documentary programme titled *Here Come the Seventies.* In the opening montage, viewers saw a man with a jet pack rise off the ground. Many viewers assumed we would all have one by the end of the decade. But fifty years later, they still haven't arrived. It's not that they don't exist. They do, but they are expensive, difficult to navigate, dangerous, and await regulatory guidelines. Can we land on a busy sidewalk? On rooftops? Will they explode? Will I rocket into a hydro wire? The market is understandably wary. But there are people in Silicon Valley working on flying cars.

In 2001, another failed transport solution arrived in the form of the Segway scooter. Before it was released into the market, the hype was considerable. Its inventors said it would change our lives; it would have a bigger impact on society than the personal computer. Then it arrived and the market deemed it expensive ($9,000 at the time), cumbersome, slower than a bicycle, and difficult to park. And it wasn't clear where we could ride one—sidewalks? Bike lanes? Roads? The fundamental problem with the Segway, one that eluded its designers, was that it didn't solve any problems. The market determined that it was essentially an expensive toy that is now used occasionally by mall police.

The average Canadian commuter spends 100 hours per year in gridlock. There must be investments in infrastructure, be it roads, public transit, or IT-related investments to optimize on traffic flows— that is, enabling smart roads and smart cities. Using data networks to channel traffic flows can optimize existing infrastructure, but this requires improvements in broadband and a more innovative ecosystem. Cities are the primary generators of wealth, and traffic congestion and the lack of alternatives are needlessly slowing us down, putting us at an even greater disadvantage to cities that have efficient systems. Let's hope we don't make the same mistake building out broadband access that we have made with transportation.

We are the only Western nation that doesn't have high-speed rail. It has been dismissed as too expensive and also a political quagmire. The most logical corridor would run from Toronto to Ottawa to Montreal to Quebec City. Calgary and Edmonton are western candidates, but the options are few and politically freighted. There has been a recent announcement from Transport Minister Omar Alghabra for a fast train connecting Toronto, Ottawa, Montreal, and Quebec City.[141] We will see if these projects come to fruition as anyone who has taken the high-speed train between London and Paris, or has visited Japan, knows it would change the way we travel between cities.

The Trudeau government has pledged $10 billion for infrastructure both to expand public transit and to make it greener. It is an excellent start, but there are decades of neglect to make up for.

Far more progress is needed to develop the infrastructure that would allow the Canadian economy and its businesses to trade into the global economy and tap into global supply chains. The Canadian Chamber of Commerce noted that "for a trading nation like Canada, the strength of its economy is closely linked to the strength of its trade corridors."[142] There is one case study highlighted in the 2017 Chamber report where the creation of the Asia Pacific Gateway and Corridor Initiative (APGCI), which provided funding for "critical trade infrastructure projects," engaged private capital. "According to

---

141 See https://www.cbc.ca/news/politics/high-frequency-rail-project-1.6090930
142 Canadian Chamber of Commerce, Canadian problems that infrastructure investment can solve. July 2017. Summary provided here: https://www.pppcouncil.ca/web/P3_Knowledge_Centre/Research/Stuck_in_Traffic_for_10_000_years__Canadian_Problems_that_Infrastructure_Investment_Can_Solve.aspx?WebsiteKey=712ad751-6689-4d4a-aa17-e9f993740a89

Transport Canada, federal funds of $1.4 billion leveraged $3.5 billion in total project funding, and the investments had a spinoff effect in private investments exceeding $14 billion." Clearly, bridging public and private capital in creative ways can enhance the competitiveness of the Canadian economy, allowing for the diversification of its global footprint away from the U.S. economy and increasingly towards the rapidly growing emerging markets. It should also be highlighted that a key recommendation made in *Towards a More Innovative Future: Insights from Canada's Natural Resources Sector* was the need for "Greater investment in the supporting infrastructure in remote areas, including transportation and telecom links."[143]

Canada's Infrastructure Bank was created to help mobilize private capital into infrastructure projects and close Canada's large and growing infrastructure gap. The debate on this policy innovation was intense, with many criticizing the involvement of the private sector and the potential proliferation of user fees. When there is private capital used in such public infrastructure projects, this requires that returns be paid to the private investors, flowing from the revenue generated from the underlying infrastructure operations. We see it in tolled highways and tolled bridges. Without the private participation in these infrastructure projects, the projects won't be undertaken— governments at all levels are far too stretched financially to deliver the needed infrastructure. Canada's infrastructure gap is growing, and there is an urgent need to address these gaps. There is little doubt that when structured appropriately public private partnerships can deliver significant value.

---

143 Public Policy Forum, Towards a more innovative future: Insights from Canada's Natural Resources Sector. 2012.

Dominic Barton noted that we need to look at the long term. "The way I think we need to look at our infrastructure gap, is more like a 30-year plan," he said. "What does the 30-year plan for Canada look like on infrastructure? And so it goes beyond any government. And just say, let's have a national conversation and consensus around what we're going to do. And not everyone is going to agree on it, but, for example, I'm a big believer in this Northern Corridor."

Many infrastructure projects impact Canada's Indigenous communities and have resulted in protests, legal challenges, and political roadblocks. Federal governments need to proactively and effectively engage these communities as partners in infrastructure projects that impact their communities to reduce frictions.

There is enough profit to benefit all stakeholders. There are indeed financial and economic structures that have been advanced that would enable Indigenous participation in large critical infrastructure projects, facilitate timely completion and provide Indigenous communities with needed resources to develop their local economies. One such example discussed above is the 3IT model, which was advanced at the 2018 CanInfra Challenge and Canadian Transformational Infrastructure Summit.[144] Meaningful engagement would also reduce risks associated with such investments in Canada and would attract much needed foreign capital.

Canada has been called a country with too much geography and not enough history. Infrastructure has always been a challenge. Physical infrastructure will always be important; goods and services and people still need to get from points A to B. But as COVID-19 demonstrated,

---

144 CanInfra Challenge. https://www.caninfra.ca/ and https://www.caninfra.ca/indigenous-infrastructure-investment-trust-3it

broadband infrastructure is increasingly critical. Yesterday we drove in to work, today we log in to work. Same exercise, just a different mode of "transportation." Canada lags on many fronts. We still have a digital divide between urban and rural subscribers. In 2017, only 37 percent of rural households had access to internet speeds of at least 50 Megabits per second. This compares to 97 percent of urban homes. Access for indigenous communities is even worse.[145] The result is a significant percentage of the population is at a distinct disadvantage. While urban users have access to the autobahn, rural people are still travelling the back roads.

There are other, more worrisome issues with Canada's digital highway though. In 2013, the House of Commons Standing Committee on Industry, Science and Technology had a hearing on the adoption of digital technologies by small and medium businesses. One of the people they heard from was Harley Finkelstein, President of Shopify, who talked about the lower e-commerce adoption rates by Canadian firms compared to the United States.[146]

A report done by software giant Salesforce noted that Canada isn't adopting new technologies at the same rate as the U.S. or other developed economies. Those that did were almost twice as likely to report strong growth over the previous three years.

Michael Geist, a law professor at the University of Ottawa and the Canada Research Chair in Internet and E-commerce Law also

---

145 Government of Canada. High-speed access for all: Canada's connectivity strategy. https://ised-isde.canada.ca/site/high-speed-internet-canada/en/canadas-connectivity-strategy/high-speed-access-all-canadas-connectivity-strategy

146 Government of Canada. Standing Committee on Industry, Science and Technology. May 7, 2013. https://www.ourcommons.ca/DocumentViewer/en/41-1/INDU/meeting-68/evidence#Int-8008856

appeared before the Standing Committee. He cited a 2011 study that showed SME (Small and Medium-sized Enterprises) use of mobile devices was low, and that many online tools—collaborative tools, application sharing, web sharing—were used by a small minority. The reasons given by small business people were: their product wasn't suited to online sales, a lack of technical know-how, lack of resources, and the fact there weren't clear benefits.[147]

"So we have a problem," Geist said to the committee. He also noted that there was a sense of déjà vu to the proceedings. The committee had already done studies of Broadband and Internet access, a study of the intellectual property regime, and a study on e-commerce. A Senate Committee on Transport and Communications did a study on the wireless sector; the Heritage Committee did a study of Entertainment software in Canada. There were government studies on privacy and social media and on cyber-bullying.

"My point," Geist said, "is that our problems with the digital economy—including SME ICT adoption—are not the result of a lack of study. These issues have been studied extensively for years."[148]

If there is a strength of our federal system, it lies in studying an issue. There are studies, inquiries, Royal Commissions. While it is laudable to give detailed attention to issues that affect society, at some point studying becomes a replacement for action. It demonstrates concern, but there is no need to actually do anything.

"At least part of the problem," Geist said, "lies in Canada's lack of a cohesive, forward-looking digital economy strategy. This failure is plainly hurting all aspects of the digital economy. It creates business

147 See https://openparliament.ca/committees/industry/41-1/72/john-connell-1/
148 See https://openparliament.ca/committees/industry/41-1/72/john-connell-1/

uncertainty, undermines consumer adoption of e-commerce, harms innovation, and sends an unmistakable signal that this is simply not a governmental priority."[149]

There are high costs and limited choice when it comes to broadband. The result is Canada lagging behind other countries. During normal times, this is a disadvantage, but when COVID-19 hit, those disadvantages were magnified. Suddenly, stores and restaurants were closed, and the world was selling everything online. Those who were the most digitally adept had the best chances of survival. The pandemic was held up as something of a black swan event, something that we couldn't have planned for. Yet, other countries did. Going back to coverage of other pandemics—SARS, H1N1—there is a consensus among epidemiologists that another one was coming. At some point, the bacteria would get it right, and it would catch on and devastate the globe. This was always a matter of when, not if. We would have to wait to see how severe, how deadly, how contagious the virus was. But its arrival was a virtual certainty.

Change has always been a constant, but now disruption is. Those societies best equipped to deal with disruption are those that are proactive, rather than reactive. Throughout our history, Canada has tended to be more cautious, to react rather than initiate. If we fail to embrace risk, we risk being left behind. The landscape that COVID-19 created was essentially Darwinian—those who adapted survived and those who failed died out.

Michael Geist wrapped up his speech to the Committee by saying, "We could talk about what a Canadian digital economy strategy that

---

149 Michael Geist, Canada has an internet problem. *Huffington Post*. https://www. huffpost.com/archive/ca/entry/geist-digital-economy_b_3353051

incorporates SME digital technology adoption would look like, including legislative reforms, educational initiatives, skills training, and commitments to increase competition and ensure access for all, but the starting point is simply to say without a digital economy strategy that weaves together these various issues, we should not be surprised by the lagging performance by Canadian SMEs. Indeed, we practically scripted it."[150]

It isn't just small business that is missing out. Inefficiency and lack of competitiveness hurt the government, which is missing out on hundreds of millions of tax dollars. In 2018, the federal government set up Innovative Solutions Canada. In the initial press release, the Ministry of Innovation, Science and Economic Development announced, "Through this program, government departments are inviting small businesses to come up with a new innovative product, service or solution in answer to specific challenges they face." The winning businesses would receive up to $150,000 to develop the idea, and up to $1 million to create a working prototype.[151] The idea was the federal government would be the first customer, helping to commercialize the product. There were nine separate challenges, ranging from agriculture to transportation. The news release was accompanied by hopeful quotes from various ministers. The Honourable Mary Ng, Minister of Small Business and Export Promotion, wrote, "Small businesses are the backbone of our economy and employ over 8 million hard-working Canadians. Innovative Solutions Canada is a

---

150 See https://openparliament.ca/committees/industry/41-1/72/john-connell-1/
151 Government of Canada, Government challenges small businesses to innovate. https://www.canada.ca/en/innovation-science-economic-development/news/2018/11/government-challenges-small-businesses-to-innovate.html

fantastic programme that uses government procurement to help small and medium-sized businesses innovate and then commercialize their innovations."

Other ministers echoed these sentiments. It was a welcome, well-intentioned initiative, but small business still needs the tools to operate in the digital economy. In 2019, Prime Minister Trudeau promised to reduce Canadians cell phone bills by 25 percent.[152] The government would consult with telecoms, encourage competition, and plan to award new wireless spectrum on the basis of consumer choice and affordability, not just the highest bids. Canada's Competition Bureau conducted a study on competition in the broadband industry. The published results were a surprise: most Canadians were happy with their internet service provider.[153]

It wasn't clear which Canadians they spoke to. On March 16, 2021, an online protest against telecoms took place. "Canadians pay some of the highest prices in the world for internet and mobile service," the rallying cry read. "It's only getting worse. The federal government and the CRTC can take steps to lower your bills. Instead, they are protecting Big Telecom's massive profits. It's time to speak out!"

Headlines announcing Canada's high rates and disgruntled customers are a regular occurrence. A *National Post* article titled "Why Canadian cell phone bills are among the most expensive on the planet," cited the industry's usual response that Canada is large and

---

152 Paula Sambo Trudeau pledges to cut Canadians' cell phone bills by 25 percent within four years. *Financial Post*, September 23, 2019. https://financialpost.com/telecom/media/trudeau-pledges-to-cut-taxes-for-middle-class-lower-phone-bills

153 Government of Canada, Delivering choice: A study of competition in Canada's broadband industry. August 7, 2019. https://www.competitionbureau.gc.ca/eic/site/cb-bc.nsf/eng/04470.html

under-populated and infrastructure costs are higher here.[154] Though Australia is a large, sprawled country, it pays less than half what Canadians do. Michael Geist offered another reason they charge what they do: "because they can." A 2008 Merrill Lynch analysis concluded that the Canadian market was the most profitable of twenty-three countries surveyed.

Infrastructure in all its many forms is going to be key to operating successfully in the 21st century. In the 19th century, we built a railway over a vast distance through hostile land and punishing conditions. Using 19th-century technology and engineering tools, it took just four years, a remarkable feat. As many people know, there are home renovations that take longer. We have the knowledge and the skills; we just need the political will.

154 Tristin Hopper, Why Canadian cell phone bills are among the most expensive on the planet. *National Post*, September 18, 2017. https://nationalpost.com/news/canada/ why-canadian-cell-phone-bills-are-among-the-most-expensive-on-the-planet

9

An Integrated Framework

The propensity to truck, barter and exchange one thing for another is common to all men, and to be found in no other race of animals.

—Adam Smith

In many ways we are at a crossroads in our history. "We are at an existential moment for this country," Amanda Lang said, "and it is playing itself out in many different spheres, which will force us to decide what we will do. The thing we haven't done is create a framework for how we consider the value of, for instance, a natural resource project. What is the framework we will use to measure its worth in terms of other commitments we have and other beliefs and goals? These are things we have to ask ourselves in a bigger picture way, and I don't think that we're doing a good job."

The pandemic, global rivalries, economic uncertainty, unprecedented technological disruption, social division, climate change, and national security concerns have both overwhelmed and numbed us. Adam Smith's quote reminds us of our unique ability as a species to trade and barter with one another. With 38 million potential traders,

Canada is poised to take to the global economic playing field like never before. We just need the right gear and game plan. Canada is a country with few enemies and a history of earned goodwill, poised to connect and trade with the world like none other. As a *Financial Times* article put it, "It is now taken as read that the world has entered an era of deglobalization as national tensions rise and global supply chains fragment. But in parts of the digital world, at least, the exact opposite is true: we are seeing the rapid acceleration of e-globalisation."[155] *We are entering the era of e-globalisation.*

We need to develop policies to unleash our potential for the next generation and empower individual Canadians to plug into and onto the new economy. We should place our biggest bet on the fact that we can earn our way to shared prosperity rather than taxing our way to that promised land. There is no doubt that we all need to pay our fair share of taxes. However, countless years fighting over a shrinking pie and potential class warfare is draining and corrosive for everyone. It also lacks imagination. Our endless discussions on taxes are pitting classes of Canadians against one another because of how we frame them. We are all entitled to ask why and for what purpose our government is taxing us. In a democracy, no government is entitled to any assumptions.

We now turn to our proposed holistic framework to allow Canada to achieve its true potential in this new technological era. The framework requires new policies that enable Canadians to unlock the key obstacles to productivity and innovation. We propose a framework based on four pillars, all operating within a frictionless ecosystem.

---

155 John Thornhill, We are entering the era of e-globalisation. *Financial Times*, February 4, 2021. https://on.ft.com/3cMKxQS

To break down the question of how best to unlock the potential of personal economic productivity and to create more prosperity over the next fifty years, it is helpful to return to our assessment of the basic building blocks of productivity and wealth creation. They haven't changed over human history: people, materials and resources, tools, and access to markets and capital, operating within a frictionless ecosystem. This framework is displayed in Figure 9. No matter when or where, these are the basic ingredients—healthy and educated people with access to tools to do productive things and the ability to obtain the materials (inputs, environment, natural resources, and intermediate inputs) and capital to produce something useful to offer others, and access to markets to sell them into. While it is absolutely necessary for governments to regulate to achieve various public policy objectives, unnecessary bureaucracy and burdensome red tape hurts us all. This is not an ideological argument about smaller or larger governments but hits at a need for the most effective form of 21st-century policies.

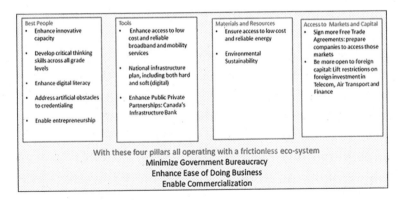

Figure 9 Pillars and policies

Pillar 1: People

People are the engines of prosperity. We have to maximize the potential and opportunity of all Canadians. We must better enable Canadians to pursue their passions, with access to capital the tools necessary to succeed, all while operating within a frictionless ecosystem. The pipeline of talent must come from both inside Canada's borders and through immigration.

To maximize the internal pipeline, Canada must invest in world-class educational and health care systems, so as to optimize the resources within Canada's borders. Canada needs the most highly educated and appropriately skilled labour force who are healthy to work. There are significant gaps in the skills needed to succeed in the 21st-century economy, including critical thinking and coding, and how well students are prepared for the enormous transition to post-secondary education and/or in demand skills training. These gaps in the educational system within Canada must be addressed if Canadian youth are to be best prepared for the 21st-century economy and if Canadians are to achieve their potential.

Immigration is absolutely necessary to support this pillar and to ensure we have a strong, diverse, and innovative economy. Not only does immigration increase Canada's numbers, and hence the size of its GDP, but diversity itself is beneficial to the Canadian economy as an engine of entrepreneurship.

A modern successful Canadian economy needs to send a clear message to the world's talent that if you have the energy and the ideas, you should come to Canada and put yourself and others to work. Innovation, prosperity, the ease of doing business and the facilitation of practicing in one's profession are critical in both the attraction and retention of the world's most talented and mobile immigrants.

The American dream is known worldwide; what is the Canadian dream? The argument has been made for decades that Canadians are risk-averse. Perhaps this was true in 1967 on Canada's 100th birthday, but it can no longer be true if we want to be prosperous on our 200th birthday.

In order for Canada to optimize its potential, there must also be a much more serious effort to engage with Canada's indigenous communities, a significant potential source of additional Canadian prosperity.

Pillar 2: Tools

The second pillar in the proposed unifying framework is access to the necessary tools needed by individuals and businesses to succeed in the modern innovation-based economy. Without these tools, Canada will not attract the best global talent, and domestic talent will be unable to achieve their full potential. Policies must be put in place to ensure these tools are ubiquitous across the economy, and without artificial and bureaucratic obstacles.

These tools include meaningful and focused investments in the right classes of infrastructure to support a modern and innovative Canadian economy, including both physical and digital infrastructure, and their integration to enable smart cities and communities.

The three critical infrastructure sectors, which all other sectors interact with—telecommunications, finance, and air transport—are highly protected and have inhibited innovation across the economy.

While protection of the banking and finance sector is justified in exchange for the stability the sector provides, such is not the case for the other protected sectors. This protection constitutes the largest impediment to Canada's ability to overcome the significant headwinds the economy faces. It is inconceivable that Canadian innovation can rise to the levels needed without significant policy changes, which eliminates such protection.

Pillar 3: Materials and Resources

The third pillar is ensuring ready access to resources and materials within the Canadian economy for individuals and businesses to leverage. Canada must efficiently and responsibly develop its natural resources and at the same time preserving, repairing, and sustaining the environment. Canada's incredible abundance and diversity of natural resources and materials must be utilized to maximize the country's wealth. It is a source of strategic advantage and must be developed and exploited in a sustainable way.

The increased intensity and frequency of storms and forest fires are examples of the additional costs associated with business practices that are not sustainable. Being environmentally conscious can create wealth. Recycling and reusing are some of the most effective cost-cutting measures available to any business willing to take the time and effort to implement them. Deploying strategies to minimize waste delivers direct financial rewards. This result is supported by the empirical evidence that shows investing into companies which are deploying sustainable strategies and are committed to achieving the world's ambitious climate goals outperform those companies that are not.

These resources and materials must be made available within Canada at global prices and, as the war in Ukraine has highlighted, Canada can have a major role to play in ensuring global energy security to our key trading partners. For example, the newly minted Canadian CEO of Shell said earlier this year that he "think[s] Canada is incredibly well placed," and that Shell was "excited by the potential" of the LNG Canada project. "There's potential for more and so Canada can play a very, very good role and it's not only the supply of LNG, it's arguably going to be amongst the most carbon efficient LNG plants anywhere in the world." With a more innovative mindset, these resources can be used to undertake more processing within Canada—this is not a call for government intervention in making this happen. Rather, increased domestic processing of Canada's vast natural resources would be the natural outcome of the policy recommendations made within this book that make the Canadian economy more innovative.

We also acknowledge the reality that the natural resource sectors still make up a significant part of the Canadian economy. However, we need more innovative solutions to be brought into Canada's natural resources sectors.

As new industries such as electric cars emerge, and many others that we may be able to predict and others that we cannot, Canadian businesses must have access to both the natural resources and material inputs needed. These innovation gaps must be addressed with urgency. As these industries of the future develop and new suppliers emerge, there is a first mover advantage. There will be many high-tech material inputs needed for electric cars and other emerging industries. The facilities needed to produce these are incredibly capital intensive. If the Canadian ecosystem is not conducive to innovation, these new companies and new facilities will locate in the United States or elsewhere. Once these investments are made, they cannot be easily undone. As these new industries emerge, and peripheral and supporting industries develop, Canada will miss out if the obstacles to innovating in Canada are not addressed.

Perrin Beatty put it perfectly: "We do this by becoming the place the world turns to for solutions to the technical, environmental and social challenges of providing people with energy, food and materials. We don't export our natural resources alone, but also disseminate the technology and knowhow to extract these resources in the right way."[156]

The framework and recommendations proposed in this book will enhance Canada's innovation ecosystem. When those recommendations are implemented, innovation within the resources sectors will also improve, and so too will the amount of processing and manufacturing of higher-value intermediate inputs. This will allow Canada to follow in the footsteps of the United States, which was originally resource-based but made a major shift to higher-value processing and innovation-based industries. Countries such as Japan, Korea, and Singapore had no resources to speak of and were forced to move up the value chain in order to survive. Canada will also need to make such a transformation as natural resources diminish in relative importance in the coming decades. With an increased focus on innovation, a natural evolution will emerge to higher-value processing within the Canadian economy.

---

156 Perrin Beatty Speaking Notes, *The Future of Canadian Natural Resources.* Premier's BC Natural Resource Forum, February 2, 2017, Prince George, British Columbia.

Pillar 4: Access to Consumer and Capital Markets

Canada must aggressively pursue free trade and investment protection agreements with more global markets. While enhanced access to these markets is necessary, it is by no means sufficient to overcome the significant headwinds facing the Canadian economy. Enhanced productivity and innovation are required in order for Canadian businesses to be prepared both to exploit opportunities in these new markets and to compete more effectively against the increased foreign competition inside Canada which would come with such trade and investment agreements.

Many of the obstacles to innovation and productivity stem from protectionist policies. Canadians are indeed able to compete and win in the global economy, provided they are given the appropriate environment to operate within and the ingredients needed. Moving away from Canada's protectionist mindset, enabling Canadian companies to be more innovative and productive, opening Canada to both more imports and inward investment, and opening markets abroad to more Canadian exports and outward foreign investment, will allow Canada to achieve its potential.

It is important to note that despite tariff exemptions within the USMCA for imports of intermediate inputs, many companies, particularly smaller ones, are unable to do the paperwork involved to take advantage of these arrangements. Despite the tariff-free access to the U.S. and Mexican markets that come with the USMCA agreement, many companies pay the non-USMCA (i.e., non-NAFTA) tariff rather than incurring the costs associated with complying with the agreement. The costs of demonstrating compliance on local content are too high and bring friction to the economy.

Canada must strive to dismantle supply management, a system of tariffs and quotas that protect domestic farmers from foreign competition. As noted in a *National Post* opinion piece, "NAFTA or not, protecting supply management is protecting an ever-dwindling number of ever-wealthier farmers."[157] It raises the price of dairy products, encouraging consumption of less healthy alternatives, especially among the poor. This arrangement puts the interest of dairy farmers above that of all other Canadians. In Canada's agreement with Europe, the Comprehensive Economic Trade Agreement, quotas were put on the imports of cheese, which means once Canadians eat a certain amount of cheese, they are then essentially forced to eat Canadian cheese.

Although we have made recent progress, Canada must also be made more open to foreign investment. Canada still has room to liberalize its foreign investment rules in the context of the needs and priorities demanded by the modern economy. Both the mandatory review for investments over the government's threshold and the sectors that have heavy restrictions on foreign ownership have hurt the Canadian economy significantly. These restrictions on foreign investment must be reduced. In the case of the review, there is evidence that it should be abolished (except for national security reviews), or at the very minimum made even more transparent. As it is currently set up, the Federal government can simply reject a potential foreign investment transaction on national security grounds, whereas the decision may come across as really for protectionist reasons. There are strong

---

157 Michael Osborne, It really is time to kick Canada's $2.6-billion dairy habit. *Financial Post*, July 6, 2018. https://business.financialpost.com/opinion/its-really-time-to-kick-canadas-2-6-billion-dairy-cartel-er-habit

arguments why almost all restrictions on foreign participation within telecom must be eliminated—there are few insurmountable economic or security justifications for many these restrictions. In the case of air transport, domestic carriers cannot hold Canadians hostage to take routes that are profitable to these incumbents but sub-optimal for Canadians. When the business case makes sense and foreign carriers are willing to offer a direct flight to an international location, they should be allowed landing rights if a domestic carrier does not offer that service. If there is sufficient demand, then both the domestic and international carriers should be allowed to offer these flights, which would enhance the quality and variety of services available, and lower prices. This would enhance connectivity, make Canadian companies more competitive, and improve Canadian trade and investment performance in the global economy.

Enhanced competition within Canada would enable Canadian firms to penetrate global markets and win. Increased Canadian innovative capacity would bring more cutting-edge exports—both within the resources sector and more broadly—and far more enduring prosperity. Recall that during the rapid rise in the value of the Canadian dollar during the 2002–2007 period, it was Canada's most innovative exports that proved most resilient.[158] With the recommendations made here, this would be the new norm for Canada—a move away from low-value exports to those that are much more innovative and advanced. Canadian firms would then be better placed to succeed in Asia, Europe, Latin America, and elsewhere. Canada's dependence

---

158 Government of Canada, Report of the Standing Senate Committee on Banking, Trade and Commerce. October 2018. https://sencanada.ca/content/sen/committee/421/BANC/reports/BANCReportImportersExporters_E.pdf

on the U.S. economy would fall and Canada can cut through the significant headwinds it faces.

A Frictionless Ecosystem

A clear need remains for government involvement at all levels to regulate the economy and business behaviour to achieve important overall public policy outcomes. This includes ensuring that banks are properly capitalized and do not expose the economy to systemic risks, and remain protected. Banks have delivered on the grand bargain. Governments must also ensure that household debt and housing price bubbles do not precipitate an economic crisis, or that doctors, dentists, and taxi drivers are properly trained and licensed. These frameworks are indeed necessary, and the economy and society overall would be far worse off without such interventions. There is no other institution with this broad perspective and ultimate public accountability to be entrusted with this mandate. In a democracy, as imperfect as it may be, at least there is a vote every four years as a check on power.

This theme was reflected in the many interviews conducted for this book. Perhaps the best example was an interview with the CEO of a company that exports to many countries. He expanded his production facility, doubling capacity. However, the opening was significantly delayed, during which the completed facility sat empty and idle, while his company negotiated with more than one level of government on the environmental front, notwithstanding the company's full legal compliance. Clearly, this reflects a government bureaucracy imposing unnecessary costs on a productive business creating jobs, capital investments, and exports, which otherwise contribute to growing the Canadian economy and tax revenue for the Canadian government.

"Canada's regulatory system is smothering business in Canada, thanks to a growing mix of complex, costly and overlapping rules from all levels of government. A report by the Canadian Chamber of Commerce, *Death by 130,000 Cuts: Improving Canada's Regulatory Competitiveness*, calls on governments to modernize their regulatory frameworks and give businesses in Canada room to thrive."[159]

What tops the World Economic Forum's annual ranking for key business challenges in Canada is an inefficient government bureaucracy, followed by high tax rates, insufficient innovation capacity, and inadequate infrastructure. Figure 10 shows that the top two reflect challenges working with government. Three and four are

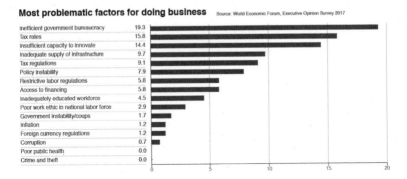

Figure 10 World Competitiveness Report, 2017–18

Source: World Economic Forum, https://www.weforum.org/reports/the-global-competitiveness-report-2017-2018/

159 Canadian Chamber of Commerce, *Death by 130,000 Cuts: Improving Canada's Regulatory Competitiveness, May 2018.* https://chamber.ca/wp-content/uploads/publications/documents/Chamber%20Site/180531DeathBy130000CutsImprovingCanadasRegulatoryCompetitiveness.pdf

challenges with both innovation and infrastructure. And the next three all involve government policy—tax regulations, policy instability, and restrictive labour regulations.

Business dislikes uncertainty. Will the government's policies change in the future? As reflected in many interviews, governments often go back through time to try and implement an alternative interpretation of legal or regulatory compliance retroactively. We heard this sentiment several times. Policy uncertainty is a significant inhibitor of companies investing in Canada, from the future of trade agreements, the likelihood of trade wars, minimum wage laws, a carbon tax, and the future of pipelines in Canada. Will future governments reverse increasing personal tax rates, or reverse falling corporate tax rates? These uncertainties hinder business decisions and make Canada less attractive as a place to undertake business.

One of the authors of this book participated in a Canadian government roundtable in the Middle East in 2016 with an ambassador and two other prominent Canadian executives. The panel was promoting Canada as a place to invest to international investors. The very first substantive question related to policy uncertainty: "If we invest in Canada, is our investment welcome?" During the debrief with many of the participants afterward, these concerns were the result of the government's unfortunate treatment of Wind Mobile. After making commitments to the foreign backers, the Canadian government reneged and forced Wind to spend millions in legal and other costs to overcome obstacles placed before them by incumbents in the telecom sector.

Upon inviting the foreign investors into Canada, the Canadian government at the time clearly signalled it had the political will to open up the sector to foreign competition. But when it came time to demonstrate this political will, the government retreated—promises for spectrum and tower sharing were never honored.[160] This has been a costly error on the part of the government and contributes to the significant policy uncertainty within Canada.

The sentiment by interviewees working to start small businesses highlighted the many regulatory hurdles, and the absence of will on the part of government officials to be helpful. The outcome of such obstacles is a stifling of the entrepreneurial spirit and innovative capacity of the economy and a diminishment in Canada's prosperity. This absolutely needs to be addressed.

The Unifying Framework

Figure 11 depicts our unifying framework, which has four pillars, operating on top of a frictionless ecosystem. It is important to note that the pillars are not mutually exclusive, as there is tremendous overlap across the pillars. With the policy recommendations made above, these four pillars will be strengthened, and operating within the frictionless ecosystem, the outcome will be enhanced innovation, enhanced productivity, and enhanced prosperity.

160 Amanda Lang and Kevin O'Leary Exchange, CBC. Wind Mobile's Naguib Sawiris Slams Canadian Duopoly & Government. November 20, 2011. https://www.youtube.com/watch?v=-g61PnQanEg

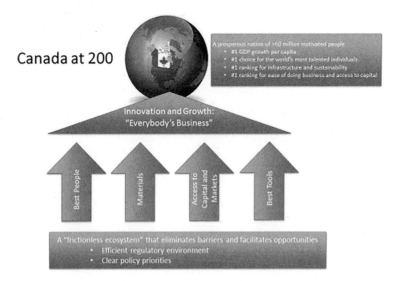

Figure 11 Canada 200 Model—Ensuring Canada remains great at 200. Rather than say #1 in all these areas, should we say top 10 in the world?

Source: Authors' conceptualization.

The book's road map for this vision requires bold policies that address challenges across all four pillars, and, at the same time, enables a frictionless economic ecosystem. Tinkering on the margins is insufficient. The headwinds facing Canada are increasing, and the longer we wait, the further Canada falls behind, and the more difficult it becomes to reverse the troubling trends. This book is a call to action for all Canadians to participate in this national conversation and form a new consensus for the new economy and for governments to act to ensure Canada remains great on its 200th birthday.

10

Conclusion

I believe the world needs more Canada.

—Bono

The global economic race is intensifying. Countries are trading places with one another on the leaderboard as technological innovation and human migration patterns challenge decades-old plans, forcing some to improvise and others to stagnate. Small economies have managed to take advantage of these realities by carving out niches, but it is harder to course-correct bigger ships. Canada is a relatively modest market in a massive land mass, complicating definitions.

The fact that other countries are surpassing Canada on incomes per person suggests that they are managing their drivers of prosperity much more successfully. The policy initiatives that governments have implemented over the past few decades to reverse this trend haven't worked. They have been marginal or cosmetic, not enough to change the momentum that is working against Canada. The policies required must break down established bureaucracies and protections built into government policy. Failure to do so will result in diminished prosperity for Canadians, which will likely accelerate in the coming decades as the technological and digital revolution continues to pick up pace.

The strategy most often put forward is to increase immigration, with the idea of having 100 million people by the turn of the next century. It would certainly result in a surge in Canada's GDP, but what impact would it have on productivity, innovation, and incomes per person? We argue that any improvement will be marginal, and the downside is it would continue Canada's innovation deficit and the Canadian prosperity discount and could also bring many transitional social issues.

This presents a conundrum for policy makers. By accelerating population growth along with similar growth in infrastructure, schools, hospitals, and other essential drivers of growth, the Canadian economy will see a commensurate acceleration in economic growth. Canada's GDP will rise. But this is simply a distraction from a more critical

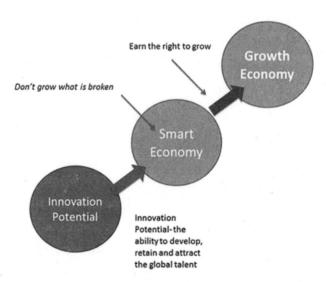

Figure 12 Sequencing and earning the right to grow

Source: Author's conceptualization.

issue—our lack of innovation and productivity. It isn't possible to successfully pursue both policies simultaneously.

Merely accelerating immigration to plug into Canada's existing ecosystem will make innovation and enhanced prosperity more difficult. Figure 12 highlights a key policy recommendation that flows from the analysis in this book. By first fixing what is wrong with Canada's innovation ecosystem, and then increasing immigration to plug into that ecosystem will deliver significant benefits. Canada must earn the right to grow.

Our Call to Action

The next fifty years will bring tremendous change. Canadian policy makers, business leaders, and all other Canadians cannot simply wish for the best. Canada's prosperity, innovation, and global influence is sliding. The economic and political implications of these trends will manifest themselves in the coming years. Incomes in Canada will continue to fall relative to global standards, and many of those great Canadian characteristics that define the country, such as health care, education, housing, tolerance, and inclusivity, will all come under strain. By implementing the changes recommended in this book, Canada can take control of its future destiny.

What Does Success Look Like?

Imagine a large, growing nation of people with a high quality of life, opportunity, and wellness. A local market with sufficient scale to encourage entrepreneurship and foster innovation in many spheres. Domestic scale-up opportunities that better prepare businesses before they go global. A country that is an attractive place to do business—with a high degree of entrepreneurial spirit, with taxation and regulatory policies that encourage rather than stifle this spirit. A frictionless ecosystem which enables entrepreneurship and innovation rather than unnecessarily impeding them. An economy where large government-protected oligopolies do not misuse their market power to extract higher prices, deliver lower quality, and inhibit innovation. An economy where artificial barriers are not in place to inhibit talented and highly skilled immigrants from practising their trade. An economy where everyone can dream and see a path to realizing their dreams.

With a more innovative and dynamic Canadian economy, Canada would be able to attract and retain the best talent. Instead of Tesla building a battery giga-factory in the United States, it instead chooses to build in Canada because of access to raw materials, a skilled labour force, outstanding infrastructure, and an efficient cost structure (energy, labour, and taxes). It could be the same for many other businesses. It's time for Canada to stop looking in the rear-view mirror—it's time to look ahead fifty years and navigate a path to continued greatness at 200 and skate with our head up to the goal and score for our future national success.

Many of the themes of this book and the potential of our continuing Canadian project were captured well by Blake Hutcheson, the CEO of Omers, as he looks ahead in managing one of the country's largest pension funds here and abroad.

"As we look to the future the best way to unlock tremendous success is not by focusing on returns and hard numbers. If leaders focus on: their most important asset, their people; their culture and brand; being forward focused embracing innovation and inclusion; and their true purpose . . . spectacular results will come. They just will. And Canada has an amazing opportunity to demonstrate this leadership formula, in a land where your handshake and reputation still mean everything, and our competitive advantages are as exciting as they are apparent. The future belongs to this great nation! And in my view our next generation of leaders will better all hopes and expectations, however lofty, that we collectively hold for them at this moment in history".

Acknowledgements

This book would not be possible without the insights and voices of leaders across our country. Our formal conversations on the topics researched in this book began with a Canadian Club panel event in 2016 with Paul Martin, Michael Wilson, David Rosenberg and Amanda Lang. This was an essential point in our research and helped identify many issues that are at the foundation of this book. The panel discussion and the reception it received confirmed the need to write this book.

We realized immediately the need to hear from Canadians across the country, to draw on their insights and vision for Canada's success. We reached out to over 200 Canadian thought leaders across the nation and beyond. We also captured the voices of emerging leaders, including over 2000 graduate students from the University of Toronto and other students from across Canada. Their time and insights are foundational to our research. Without the thousands of hours they collectively provided, we would not have been able to develop the insights in this book, including where Canada currently stands, the head winds Canada faces, whether Canada is well prepared to navigate its path over the coming century, and ultimately the pathway and the framework this book lays out to a prosperous Canada at 200.

We also acknowledge the extensive support of Dr. Susan Murray, Daniela Stratulativ, Ritesh Mehta and a large number of students from the University of Toronto, including Phil Gazaleh; Maria Fakhruddin; Daniel Hart; Laila Jaunkalns; Steven Lampert; Michael Amiraslani; Rebecca Patrick; Mieka Buckley-Pearson, Maggie Head, and David C. Clarke. Their excellent research and technical skills were essential in the analyses undertaken for this book.

We also thank Don Gilmour and John Tilak, both of whom spent extensive efforts on helping to shape the arguments laid out in the book. We also thank Ken Whyte and Michael Levine for their partnership to bring this book to you.

The generous financial support of the Rotman School of Management and the Rotman Institute for International Business is gratefully acknowledged. Professors Ignatius Horstmann, Bernardo Blum, Wendy Dobson, Laurence Booth and George Georgopoulos provided extensive feedback to which we are very thankful. Kevin Foley and Doug McCutcheon provided very detailed and extensive feedback on earlier drafts of this book.

Of course, for the three of us, the support of our families is at the heart of what we do. The Assaf family—Lisa and Mohamad, Danya, Zain and Hannah; the Hejazi family—Mona, Mohammed, Oussama and Khaled; and the Manget family—Christina, Amanda and Vincent and all of our parents. Thank you all for your constant support.

We wrote this book because of our love for this country, for our families, including our children whom we want, along with all Canadians, to inherit a country with even greater promise and prosperity than we inherited from our parents.